D1470062

THE MARRIAGE
REPAIR KIT

THE MARRIAGE REPAIR KIT

Bob Moorehead, Sr.

Wolgemuth & Hyatt, Publishers, Inc.
Brentwood, Tennessee

© 1988 by Bob Moorehead, Sr.
All rights reserved. Published September, 1988. First edition.

No part of this publication may be reproduced, stored in a
retrieval system, or transmitted in any form by any means,
electronic, mechanical, photocopy, recording, or otherwise,
without the prior written permission of the publisher, except
for brief quotations in critical reviews or articles.

Unless otherwise noted, the Bible version used in this publication
is The Holy Bible: New International Version. Copyright © 1973,
1978, 1984 International Bible Society. Used by permission of
Zondervan Bible Publishers.

Quotations noted *RSV* are from the Revised Standard Version of
the Bible, copyrighted 1946, 1952, © 1971, 1973 by the Division
of Christian Education of the National Council of Churches of
Christ in the U.S.A. and used by permission.

Quotations noted Phillips are from J. B. Phillips: THE NEW TESTAMENT
IN MODERN ENGLISH, Revised Edition. © J. B. Phillips 1958, 1960,
1972. Used by permission of Macmillan Publishing Co., Inc.

Wolgemuth & Hyatt, Publishers, Inc.
P.O. Box 1941, Brentwood, Tennessee 37027.

Printed in the United States of America.

ISBN 0-943497-30-2

CONTENTS

that Your Body Belongs to Your Mate / Talk Freely to Each
Other about Your Sexual Frustrations / Settle Conflicts in
Other Areas Before Having Sex / Don't Use Withholding
Sex as a Club to Get Your Way / See the Sex Act as an Act
of Giving, Not Receiving / Keep the Intimacy of Your Marital
Sex a Private Thing / Do Nothing Sexually that Is Against
Your Spouse's Scruples / Avoid All Artificial Eroticism to
Stimulate Your Sex Life / Stay Sexually True to Your
Partner Both Mentally and Physically

FOREWORD

Bob Moorehead has a pastor's heart, and it clearly shows in this book. He has been there to see and feel the hurts and frustrations of Christian marriages.

His church is growing, one of the largest in the Northwest, but he talks like he is across the table from you! Bob's like that—the size of his ministry has not quenched his love for the individual, nor his desire to help where he can.

The strongest word for this book is "practical." It takes the truths of the Bible and shows how they can be applied to your marriage. Bob is "down to earth" in his approach to life and ministry. He is easy to be with, and tries not to intimidate or overpower you. I sense his humanity as well as his intense desire to serve the Lord.

I believe Bob cares. He may not have the time or opportunity to touch all the lives he may desire personally to affect, but this book will extend his compassion to many people. I pray it will have a wide audience and be mightily used of the Lord to affect the thousands of broken hearts and marriages that need the healing touch of our Lord.

Dr. David Hocking, Pastor
Calvary Church, Santa Ana, California
Speaker on "The Biola Hour" radio program

INTRODUCTION

Why another book on marriage? Isn't there a plethora of books that have been published in the last few years providing all kinds of answers to the matrimonial muddle of our times? The answer is, "yes." Some excellent books have been written and have offered great help in times of trouble.

Then why another book? After more than thirty years of counseling couples who have come on "hard times" in their marriages, I have picked up a common pattern in them all. Most marriages that need help are in need of simple repair, not total renovation. Even the severe cases began their journey to despair with mild cracks here and there, a screw that needed simply to be tightened down, or with a slipped knot that simply needed cinching up.

If you retrace the tempestuous journey of every broken marriage today, you'll discover that it moved through five basic stages: DELIGHT, DISAPPOINTMENT, DELUSION, and DESPAIR, then DIVORCE. This book will deal primarily with how people move from delight to disappointment, then on into delusion.

No one denies that as never before the family and institution of marriage are under severe attack today. At the root and core of every social ill of our society today lies the distorted family! And behind that you will find marriages that are in great need of repair.

I remember as a young boy having my first bicycle, which, of course, had tube-type tires. Flat tires occurred often. Because I couldn't afford the luxury of having my flats repaired at the service station, I bought a little tire repair kit from the local bicycle shop. The little cylindrical box contained only two items—a vulcanized substance, and some highly potent clear glue. The lid of the box provided a rough surface with which I rubbed the tube to get the patch and glue to stick.

The manufacturer of that little repair kit made millions. I've often looked back on that and thought, "Wouldn't it be wonderful if someone could manufacture a repair kit for marriages that have gone flat!" What would go in such a kit? Every marriage in need of repair is not broken in the same place, yet there are some common ills and common breaks that demand common, universal repairs. Thus, this book.

Marriages that need radical repair didn't get the way they are overnight, or even in a week. It's a very subtle, slow process that occurs until one day a spouse awakens and realizes, "We're in trouble!"

It reminds me of the proverbial case of the man who was going bald. He kept losing hair through the years, until he got down to one hair that stayed right in the middle of the top of his head. Awaking one morning, he looked on his pillow, and there it lay. He sat up in bed and exclaimed, "Great Scott, I'm bald!"

No, it just doesn't work that way. Few people just awake some morning and say, "Great Scott, my marriage is broken!"

I hear often that marriages in the 20th century are undergoing pressures that other generations never faced. Without denying the pressure caused by the complexity of our society, I really doubt that is true.

When you stop and think that only two or three generations back, marriages were under much greater pressures. The average couple had eight children. What they didn't have was any kind of washing machine, dishwasher, running water, electricity, natural gas, indoor plumbing, disposable diaper, refrigerator, television, frozen dinner, microwave oven, clothes dryer, wash-'n-wear clothes, store-bought clothes, crockpots, blenders, or fast-food restaurants. The wife's full-time career was that of being a wife and mother—running the household, gathering the eggs, milking the cows, churning the butter, sewing the clothes, darning the socks, canning the vegetables, pumping the water, and washing the clothes by hand! The husband's career was planting, cultivating, then harvesting the crop, trading, and keeping the place in good repair. The divorce rate was much lower; child delinquency was all but nonexistent; and the one thing that salvaged the family was a common cause—SURVIVAL! So I think it's stretching the point just a bit to say that marriages today have more pressure than their forefathers'.

I trust you'll find the following pages humorous, provocative, insightful, stimulating, but most of all useful. I hope if your own marriage is showing some cracks here and there, maybe some dents or bruises, you'll use this repair kit. It is intended as much as a preventative measure as it is a corrective one.

The Bible makes it abundantly clear that marriage is of God. It's not a product of the world. The world didn't create it. It only seeks to damage it. Because God alone created it, God alone can repair it when we, by disobedience or ignorance, put it in a state of disrepair.

The couples mentioned in the chapters are real people who had real problems. Only their names were changed to conceal identity.

O N E

REDISCOVERING
THE ORIGINAL

It was written right on the side of the box in bold red letters: IF UNIT IS IN NEED OF REPAIR UPON OPENING
BOX, PLEASE RETURN TO MANUFACTURER. The com-
pany that manufactured that VCR unit was delivering a message; they intended me to find their product in the state it was
when it was first manufactured. Fortunately, it was in good
working order, so there was no need to return it.

Wouldn't it be wonderful if every time we unwrapped a
marriage that was "damaged in shipment," we could send it
back to the Divine Manufacturer and get a new one from
Him? It isn't quite that easy.

Certainly, a book on marriage repair would be incomplete
if we failed to at least explore the dimensions of marriage as
God created and intended it to be. Before looking at those
precise dimensions; however, it behooves us to express some
common assumptions that are safe to express.

First of all, marriage is the first, and thus the oldest, institution of man. That says much about its importance and
priority. It came before governments, laws, the Tabernacle,
the Temple, the church, the synagogue—and long before any
sociological structure. Another assumption is that whatever
state marriage may be in today, it's a far cry from what God
intended when He drew up the plan originally. Another safe
assumption is that you are probably reading this book, not

because your marriage is in total shambles, but because you
know there are some broken areas that need repair. Your goal
is to develop or rediscover a fulfilling relationship. The last
assumption before getting down to specifics concerning the
perimeters of marriage is that no matter what damage has
been done in any marriage relationship, there is hope because
of what God can and will do. There is always hope in Christ.

There are some definite qualities of marriage we need to
uncover. If for no other reason, we need to hold them up as
the standard against which we can measure what is "passing"
for marriage today. Just briefly, let's rediscover the original
pattern. It's seen in several distinct areas.

The Mark of Severance

You don't hear or read much about this aspect of marriage. But if we're going to look at a pattern for marriage,
let's make sure we hold up the original plan. It calls for severance first.

> For this reason, a man will *leave* his father and mother and
> be united to his wife (Genesis 2:24).

There can be no "cleaving" until there has been a definite
leaving! Jesus reechoed these familiar words in Matthew 19:5
during his teaching to the Pharisees on marriage, divorce, and
remarriage.

Severance is not just physical. Obviously when two people marry, they physically become detached from their parents (hopefully!), but there is an emotional severance that
must take place. It means that their first loyalty and commitment is no longer to parent, but to spouse. It is sometimes referred to as "severing the umbilical cord." It means that their
first human love now goes to spouse, not parents. Their
whole object of relationship changes from parents to spouse.

If either spouse ever has to choose between spouse and parents, they unquestionably choose spouse. This is not a matter of cruelty, for parents should still be honored, but a matter of priority. Without the mark of severance, few marriages make it. Severance implies no disrespect but rather acknowledges that marriage demands a shift in priorities.

The Mark of Unity

Marriage is the only place where one plus one equals one in a very unique way that lets individuals blend together without losing their identity!

> So the Lord God caused the man to fall into a deep sleep; and while he was sleeping, He took one of the man's ribs and closed up the place with flesh. Then the Lord God made a woman from the rib He had taken out of the man, and He brought her to the man. The man said, "This is now bone of my bones and flesh of my flesh" (Genesis 2:21-23).

In verse 24 of that same chapter it says, "and they will become one flesh." If you want to guard, protect, and enshrine your individuality, don't get married! There is a merger that takes place in God's plan of marriage, but your individuality is not expunged, only refined.

One of the most damaging phrases I hear today among some married people is, "I just want my space." If you're married, your space is in and with your mate. That doesn't mean, of course, there aren't times when you want to be alone to think and meditate, or even have fellowship with someone else of the same sex. We are not talking about possessive/obsessive closeness. But it does, indeed, mean that you have become one with your spouse—your individual space is no longer of chief importance.

Most people overlook the fact that when God decided to create man's spouse, He used material taken right out of man. The significance of that is clear. She was designed to be part of him, and he part of her. The problem today is that many couples want a "single" kind of marriage, where a spirit of independence can prevail even after marriage. That is not a part of God's original game plan. While retaining your character and identity, one plus one is always one in marriage.

The Mark of Intimacy

The Bible says of that first couple: "The man and his wife were both naked, and they felt no shame" (Genesis 2:25). No shame. Intimacy! They were sexually joined as well as emotionally. They weren't ashamed with each other. Why? Because God's game plan was for couples to enjoy physical and emotional intimacy without shame. Shame implies guilt, and there was no guilt associated with this God-created intimacy.

The Bible teaches four truths about intimacy.

1. There is no place in marriage for extra-marital sex (see 1 Corinthians 7:2-5).

2. Each partner needs to be concerned with how to satisfy and fulfill his partner's desires, not his own.

3. There needs to be a forfeiture of one's rights (see 1 Corinthians 7:4).

4. Intimacy should be uninterrupted.

In other words, if couples must be separated for a short time, let them come back together again. Physical separation can be one of the most devastating things in any marriage. The current trend occurring in the work place of America where married couples have separate careers in separate cities trying to maintain their marriages on week-ends and holidays is a disaster. God never intended prolonged separation in any marriage relationship. The Scripture is so clear at this point.

Do not deprive each other except by mutual consent and for a time, so that you may devote yourselves to prayer. Then come together again so that Satan will not tempt you because of your lack of self control (1 Corinthians 7:5).

Paul most definitely is referring to the physical and emotional relationship in marriage here.

If you really want to know what true Biblical intimacy is in marriage, read Song of Solomon 5:10-15 to get a picture of a wife's description of her husband. Then read chapter 7, verses 1-9 to get the husband's perspective. Take a deep breath before reading, however; it's powerful!

The Mark of Permanence

When historians read about our present generation a hundred years from now, I believe they will call it the "cartridge throw-away generation." The repair business has gone by the board. Today it's "throw away the old cartridge and get a new one." The disposable diaper business is a howling success today! Unfortunately, this philosophy has been transferred to the area of marriage. If it doesn't work out, pitch it! Go for a new one!

I recently read with dismay about a Hollywood jewelry store with a sign in its window which read: WE RENT WEDDING RINGS. Somehow that doesn't have the sound of permanence in it. Of course when you realize that the usual or ordinary Hollywood stars go through an average of four marriages during their lifetime, that jewelry store probably does a land-office business in its ring rental department. It is encouraging to note that marriages are faring a little better in America at this writing. But when almost one out of two marriages that takes place in the United States ends in divorce within five years, we aren't there yet. Marriage repair shops are still full (or should be!).

In stark contrast to the current "transient" nature of marriage, what was the original game plan in this particular department of marriage? You get the drift, I think, when you read verses like this: "and be united to his wife" (Genesis 2:24).

The Hebrew word for "united" means far more than just legally connected or emotionally attached. It is the word describing an irrevocable contract, a noncancelable policy. We get a slight taste of this word if we describe gluing two pieces of India paper with super glue, then trying to separate them in ten minutes! Try it without doing irreparable damage to both pieces of paper. To separate the two sheets is to destroy.

Jesus described the word "united" when he said:

> They are no longer two, but one. Therefore what God has joined together, let man not separate (Matthew 19:6).

The word for "separate" here is the word translated "leaves" in 1 Corinthians 7:15 where it speaks of an unbeliever "leaving" his spouse. The word means divorce. So God's game plan for marriage is permanence until death.

Yes, I'm aware of the "exception clause" Jesus gave concerning cases where divorce is permissible if adultery is involved (Matthew 5:31-32) but it is never commanded, only permitted (because of the hardness of their hearts.) I strongly believe that the responsibility to forgive and reconcile takes precedence over the right to divorce because of adultery.

Jesus made it very clear later in the Matthew 19 passage (when pressed to endorse divorce because Moses had permitted it under certain circumstances), "But it was not this way from the beginning" (Matthew 19:8).

Remember the wedding vows do not read "Until debt do us part, or until lack of communication do us part, or until your physical appearance changes," but until DEATH do us part!

In the midst of World War II when Britain was being bombed and ravaged, many in England were delivering the message to

Winston Churchill to surrender. He went on national radio, and his famous words are remembered by all of England to this day:

"Wars are not won by evacuations!"

May I reverently add: NEITHER ARE MARITAL BATTLES!

We are told in Malachi 2 that marriage is a covenant. Here the Bible refers to the wife in a marriage as "the wife of your marriage covenant" (vs. 14). That passage goes on to say that God has made them one—not only in flesh, but in spirit. The plea is made in that passage not to break faith with your wife. God had no "escape clause" in His original marriage contract. Escape clauses are the inventions of men who in their depravity see marriage as no different from any other contract made to be broken.

The Mark of Response-Ability

Maybe you've never seen this word spelled exactly that way. That spelling is only valid in the institution of marriage. In spite of what a humanistic society has done to change the nature of marriage, in its original form, marriage, like anything else God ever created, has a structure. God never intended that it be tampered with architecturally! The blueprint was sketched in permanent ink. Not even the modern "white-out" can cover it.

In God's structure of marriage there are two types of responsibilities, the wife's and the husband's. Sometimes these are called "roles." I believe they are responses.

Looking at them individually, let's begin with the wife's response-ability. She has only one responsibility, to submit to her husband as the head of her and of her marriage. What does that mean? Let's read it exactly as the Bible states it because it is diametrically opposed to the prevailing philosophy today:

Wives, submit to your husbands as to the Lord. For the husband is the head of the wife as Christ is the head of the Church, His body, of which He is the Savior. Now as the Church submits to Christ, so also wives should submit to their husbands in everything (Ephesians 5:22-24).

To better understand God's structure, look at what Paul said in another place:

Now I want you to realize that the head of every man is Christ, and the head of the woman is man, and the head of Christ is God (1 Corinthians 11:3).

In marriage, God's head of authority is the man. That's the way He designed it. Now what exactly does that mean, and what are the implications of it for now? Simply put, it is a once-for-all acknowledgement on the part of the wife that God has designated her husband to be the head and authority of her and her marriage or servant-leader as Christ demonstrated in John 13. This is often referred to as "the chain of command." The little phrase does not mean that the wife is in chains and the husband is more important than the wife, or that he is in some way superior to her in value or worth. It does mean, however, that he is perceived, acknowledged, and appointed as the place where the "buck stops." He is to know her and love her and be her servant-leader. In Colossians 3:18 it says, "Wives, submit to your husband, as is fitting in the Lord." Note "as is FITTING"! In other words, it's normal, right, and natural from God's perspective to have this kind of relationship in marriage.

Submission, remember, is to a loving husband, not to a tyrant who is bent on the wife's destruction. God is never giving His permission for despotism or sin. Without the God-given head, wives quickly lose direction. Submission to a loving head—in this case, a husband—is not bondage, but freedom. It's not confinement, but release. It's not "cramping" the wife's style, or stripping her of her God-given individuality, but rather fulfilling it. A husband should give worth, substance, and meaning to his wife's being.

Some of you wives reading this may say, "But you don't know my husband," or "What do you do if you have a non-Christian husband?" First Peter 3:1-6 really speaks to that issue plainly. And, by the way, God never intended that you submit to anything ungodly, vulgar, or anything else that is morally and Biblically wrong. But don't try to change your husband. You must love him, and let God change him.

So, wives, your response-ability is simple and clear, in the translation of J. B. Phillips:

> You wives must learn to adapt yourselves to your husbands . . . (Ephesians 5:22).

"But," you ask, "what if he's wrong in some of his decisions?" Remember, he must bear the responsibility for his decisions, not you.

Now, what is the husband's response-ability? We go to the same page, chapter, and theme in the Bible.

> Husbands, love your wives, just as Christ loved the Church and gave Himself up for her to make her holy, cleansing her by washing with water through the Word, and to present her to Himself as a radiant Church, without stain or wrinkle or any other blemish, but holy and blameless. In the same way, husbands ought to love their wives as their own bodies. He who loves his wife loves himself. After all, no one ever hated his own body, but he feeds and cares for it, just as Christ does the Church (Ephesians 5:25-29).

Wow! What a mouthful! What in the world is that all about? Succinctly put, here the Bible lays down the husband's one and only response-ability—Love your wives in the same way Christ loved the Church! A big order, indeed. Let's break it down for clarity and punch. If you read the above verses very carefully and slowly, you'll see a total of five ways in which a husband is to love his wife. We might even call them five kinds of love.

A Sacrificing Love (vs. 25)

How did Christ love the church? He gave Himself up for her. When a husband loves his wife like that, enough to die for her, he's loving his wife like Christ loved the church. What does a sacrificial love do? It goes the limit, pays the price, suffers the loss, endures the inconvenience, and bears the pain. It does whatever is good, because it is a love that is un-conditional—to the point of death if need be. One should submit to a love like that!

A Holy and Cleansing Love (vs. 26)

The husband is to extend a love to his wife that is com-mitted to making holiness and purity its object. The verse says, "to make her holy, cleansing her." Most husbands do not know that their God-given response-ability is to be in the business of sanctifying their wives. In fact, one husband said to me once, "I thought God took care of that department." Well, of course, He does! It is God who cleanses us from all sin and places us in a position of salvation. He does that to males and females alike. But the husband has a role to play in this area as well. How, practically, can you as a husband carry out this command? It is done by being a role model in holiness yourself, by speaking words that are holy and sancti-fying to her, and by protecting her from the smut and filth in-herent in the world system. No husband, for example, who really wants to love his wife in this way will be involved with pornographic materials, nor will he speak base and vulgar things in her presence (or out of it). He will, in fact, be the leader in taking both himself and his wife deeper into God's holiness. Remember this is God's plan.

A Nourishing Love (vs. 29)

When a husband is loving his wife like Christ loved the church, he is careful to keep her properly nourished. I'm not talking about physical nourishment, even though that is part of his response-ability, but spiritual nourishment. Verse 29 says, He "feeds." That means he takes the initiative of imparting to his wife spiritual meat from God's Word. That doesn't necessarily imply that he's to conduct a Bible class every evening where he is the teacher and his wife is the student with attendance required! Christ did not "Lord" it over His disciples, though He could have. It means that both formally and informally he looks for ways of building his wife up in the faith. It may be no more than sharing with her, on occasion, what he gleaned from his morning devotions, or sharing a new insight he discovered while reading a book of the Bible. Husband love is the kind of love that is constantly interested in taking the wife deeper in her understanding of God's will and Word.

Caring Love (vs. 29)

"And cares" He loves his wife like he loves his own body. A person cares greatly for his own body. He showers his body, combs his hair, feeds his body, and generally takes good care of it. What is a caring love? Some translations appropriately insert "cherishing" here. When you cherish something, you set it apart, maybe place it on a pedestal, and mark it for something special. We don't treat paper drinking cups with the same care with which we treat French crystal. We "cherish" the crystal by placing it in a lovely china cabinet and by locking it up. It costs infinitely more than a paper cup!

In over thirty years of marriage counseling, the chief complaint I've heard from wives is, "I don't seem to be special to him." Caring love on the part of husbands says, "You count! You matter! You're important, vital, essential to me."

A Respectful Love (1 Peter 3:7)

Give honor to whom honor is due. It is due a husband's wife. Peter said it so as to make it abundantly clear:

> Husbands, in the same way be considerate as you live with your wives, and treat them with respect as the weaker partner and as heirs with you of the gracious gift of life, so that nothing will hinder your prayers (1 Peter 3:7).

First, there is a call for consideration. Then, there is a command to treat wives with respect. Some men treat their secretaries with more respect than their wives. Respect means giving proper adulations, compliments, making sure they know that you notice.

Note that passage says "as the weaker sex." If the wife is the weaker sex, who is the "weak" sex by comparison? Obviously, the husband! That means men are to treat their wives, not as men who are superior with no weaknesses, ministering to a weak mate, but ministering (to the weaker) as one who is weak (and knows it). Again, think of Christ, who was not weak, but who became weak for our sakes.

So, that's a picture of the product before repair was ever needed. The picture is a submissive wife and a loving husband. Now here's the clue that makes it a workable relationship. It's relatively easy to be submissive to a loving husband; it's also easy to love a submissive wife. One caution—nowhere in all of the Bible is a wife commanded to get her husband to properly love her. Also nowhere in the Bible is a husband commanded to demand that his wife be properly submissive to him. It's very clear from Scripture that each spouse is to concentrate on his or her own RESPONSE-ABILITY.

When the layers are peeled away from marriages in need of repair, usually it is discovered that the root cause is a partial or total breakdown in the response-ability area of a wife or husband. There are no shortcuts or substitutes. To be successful, we must stay with the Manufacturer's original specifications.

Now, let's take a look at some specific needed repairs, and, hopefully, reveal the part of your marriage that needs some repair.

Questions for Discussion

1. What areas of twentieth century marriage differ most significantly from marriage as God intended it? List at least three or four major areas.

2. What are some practical ways spouses can "pull off" the severance part of marriage?

3. Practically, how can you affirm Biblical unity with your spouse, yet not smother individuality?

4. Do you agree that the goal of sexual intimacy in marriage is to bring pleasure to your spouse, not "get" pleasure? What are some practical things you can do to insure that it stays that way?

5. Why do you think "permanence" in marriage has gone by the wayside today? What can practically be done to insure the permanence of your own marriage and the marriage of your children?

6. Why is headship in marriage so controversial today? Why is headship and accepting the Biblical structure of marriage so essential? What is Christ's example of headship?

7. Who has the greatest difficulty carrying out their "roles" in marriage—the husband or wife? Explain why.

Project

- Read together Ephesians 5:21-33

- Pray out loud separately:

Husband: "Lord, I recognize and accept my role to love (*wife's name*) like Christ loves the Church. I know that means loving her with a sacrificial, pure, nourishing and cherishing kind of love. I make a promise right now, with Your help, Lord, to love (_____) in that way."

Wife: "Lord, I too recognize and accept my role in our marriage, to be in submission to (*husband's name*), to recognize him as the covering, authority, and head you've given me. With Your help, I commit myself to You and to him to carry out that role as You desire."

Amen.

T W O

REVISING
THE AGENDA

Kevin and Marcy had all the appearances of a "show-window" marriage. A former football player, Kevin's large build and blonde hair said to anyone who looked, "He's all man." Marcy was bright, attractive, and the epitome of an extrovert. Her bubbly spirit and charming smile left no one guessing why Kevin picked her to be his bride some seven years earlier.

But, like many marriages of five to seven years, theirs was showing signs of wear and tear in an area that has been called the "subtlest culprit of all." They had major problems in the "priority department."

Their story I had heard many times before, but the names and dates were different. She began in our initial interview, blurting out in sobs and tears, "I don't think Kevin loves me anymore. He would probably get along just as well if I weren't around."

True to his male ego, Kevin interrupted, "That's all I've heard for weeks now — that I don't care for her anymore, and I really do! How do I convince her, preacher?" Well, the symptoms were all there. What I suspected earlier in the session was soon confirmed. Kevin was "on his way up" the corporate ladder. Nine-hour days were common, with golf on Saturday and often flights out on Sunday afternoon to other cities "to pedal his wares." Marcy felt abandoned, shut out, avoided. She felt unnecessary at times. She and her three-year-old boy were two lonely people hoping to get put back on the "agenda" by their husband and father.

Someone has quipped, "Most of our actions are really re-actions to others whose actions are also reactions." It sounds confusing but, oh, so true. Kevin's absence and increasing disinterest when he was at home had caused Marcy to "react" with feelings of neglect, indifference, and noninvolvement. To break the cycle, someone had to act—and act fast.

If you have ever driven your car through a diagnostic test, you are faced with all kinds of fancy equipment, gauges, whistles, and bells. If your car is like mine, it usually fails most of the test. The test, however, does show you the area where the real trouble exists. Most marriages that pull into a "diagnostic center" discover that the area of priorities is often the culprit causing sluggishness and poor performance.

When Kevin and Marcy were finished with their first interview, the test revealed this was exactly what their problem was; priorities were inverted and disarranged—constantly in a state of flux. It's no wonder Marcy never knew where she stood on Kevin's scale of values.

In his case, his priority list went like this (one being the most important):

1. Job—pleasing the boss

2. Hobbies—golf, tennis, and horses

3. Money—investments, etc.

4. Marcy

5. Church

6. Christ

Need I say anymore? I think you get the point, but it would be a short chapter if we stopped here.

At least the repair job is simple; we know what needs to be done. Doing it is another matter. Because most men tend to be the gregarious sort, they seldom think about where they stand in their wife's scale of values. Very few men really struggle in this area. But many women (being by temperament dependent, loving, and giving) are very much concerned about this area. Most women can live without a lot of things, but being first in their husband's scale of values isn't one they are willing to sacrifice.

Let's rearrange Kevin's scale of priorities to reflect those of the Architect who drew the original plans. Remember, for now we're doing this from the husband's point of view.

1. Jesus Christ

2. Wife

3. Children

4. Church

5. Vocation

6. Hobbies and recreation

From a humanistic standpoint, the above list given in sequential order appears out of balance. Why, everyone knows we need to look out for number one; and surely number six on that list ought to be further up the ladder than it is. How dare anyone put one's vocation—his very livelihood—as number five? I mean . . . really . . . isn't that priority list a little unrealistic? Let's see.

For the Christian husband, the number one priority is his relationship to Jesus Christ. If that isn't in proper place, it really won't matter much where those below it are placed. Jesus said,

> But seek first his kingdom and his righteousness (Matthew 6:33).

Jesus doesn't want all of your time, all of your money, or all of your interests; He just wants to come first, ahead of everything else.

Your wife is number two. When a Christian man puts Jesus first, his wife really has more of a first place than if a non-Christian man puts his wife in first place. It's the Lord alone who enables a man to give his wife high priority. What does this mean? It certainly means more than just telling her she's number two, and because of that, she should try harder! It's letting her know by the time you spend with her, by the communication you share with her, by the little favors you daily do for her—she's up at the top. It means including her in your plans, involving her in your projects, informing her about your activities, and inspiring her by a continual show of affection. It's letting her know she counts, she matters, she's important. It's that "cherishing" we've already mentioned. It's "showing her off" instead of shunning her presence, it's bragging about her sewing, her cooking, her looks, her art work. It's building her up when others are present and when they're not. It's often surprising her with a small gift, a favor, a suggestion, a comment or indulgence. It's taking the bus to work because she needs the car. Whatever it takes . . . it means a willingness to be inconvenienced, if need be, for her welfare. Most women can live without a lot; but they can't survive long without knowing they're extremely vital to you.

When the Lord and the wife are at the top of the list, then there is wholesome time and space for the children, for church, for vocation, and for hobbies.

Most marriages in need of repair must begin with getting the priorities back in proper balance. What steps are needed for this piece of repair work?

1. Examine Your Date Book.

What or who are your "time robbers"? What are you do-ing in the evenings that could be done some other time so as not to snatch your presence away from home with your wife?

Are you "scheduling" into your calendar quality and quantity time alone with your wife? Are you scheduling into your book a dinner date now and then? How about an occa-sional overnighter—even if it is just a few miles to the next town for dinner and overnight in a motel? If you're spending more time with the guys at the tennis court or racquetball court, it's time for major revisions.

2. Make Plans to "Shore Up" Inadequate Areas.

If you don't already know, find out what your wife's greatest insecurity is. In order to let her know how valuable she is, jump in and shore up that area by giving her encour-agement. For example, if she feels inadequate in the area of home decorating, suggest she attend a workshop on that topic. If she feels ill-informed about your vocation, spend some time with her acquainting her with what you do. If she feels like a failure as a cook, offer her cooking school, per-haps a special cuisine. Let her know you have a desire to see her pleased and confident in her role as a wife and mother.

3. Include Her in Dreams for the Future.

Nothing pleases a woman more in the "esteem depart-ment" than to know her husband has a high enough opinion of her to involve and include her in his plans for the future so that it becomes "our" plans. And not just as an afterthought either. This destroys the myth that the man makes all the de-cisions, then passes them down to his wife, who doesn't have the ability to think wisely or to contribute anything. Honor her ideas! Learn to listen carefully. Here is perhaps the greatest principle of all: Do to others (your wife) what you would have them do to you.

4. Release Adequate Responsibility.

Every wife feels needed, necessary, important, and valuable to her husband when he is willing to allow her an adequate amount of responsibility. Some husbands are "threatened" by this. Many women do a much better job of handling the bill paying and keeping the checkbook balanced. Yet many men "hog" that job in the home for fear of losing control, and thereby inflict upon their spouse a sense of not being needed or trusted. It really boils down to an issue of trust and confidence in his wife on the part of the husband. Because some husbands manifest little or no confidence in their wive's ability to do anything, many wives feel like "factory rejects."

Solomon spoke clearly to this when he said,

A wife of noble character, who can find? . . . Her husband has full confidence in her (Proverbs 31:10-11).

Nothing is more demeaning or frustrating than to feel that your mate doesn't have enough confidence in you even for the menial "housekeeping" duties of marriage. By the way, it works in the reverse. Wives need to be fully trusting of their husbands, even if they fail in their responsibility.

5. Build Up by Affirmation.

There is a popular myth that is mostly fostered by men today that says, "Some people may need to be stroked, but I certainly don't need that sort of thing." Everyone needs strokes, whether they admit it or not. If a husband is going to get his priorities in place, he needs to affirm his wife often and with positiveness. How? First, by verbalizing to her that she's doing a good job. The Bible talks much about building one another up in the Lord. I'm convinced that part of that is building our marriage partners up, especially the husband to the wife. Secondly, a man builds up his wife by admitting his own deficiencies as he becomes aware of them. No, it's not a sign of weakness. Many wives live day-in and day-out with a "Mr. Perfect," who never does anything wrong or makes a bad decision. Admission of weaknesses or limitations is a sign of maturity and strength.

Further, affirmation comes by planned rewards. If you are a husband reading this book, let me ask you, when was the last time you took your wife in your arms and said, "Honey, you have done such an outstanding job with the bills this month, you deserve a hot fudge sundae . . . let's go!"? It doesn't even have to be an elaborate affair, just done consistently showing affection and appreciation.

6. Clear Time for a Getaway.

What is a "getaway"? It is a spontaneous time (yet planned by you, the husband) to take your wife away for overnight, or a week-end. Go to a place away from your house where the two of you can be alone. It may be 30 miles to the next town and motel accommodations; it may be to a lodge or a resort. Maybe it's a trip to a nice downtown hotel. But, it's away, and it's your idea.

Why a getaway? It's a symbol of appreciation. It's proof that you really do want to spend some quality time with her. It confirms in her mind that she counts — matters enough that you've placed such an event on your calendar just as you would a business trip or sales meeting. Getaways occasionally can break the tight tension that so easily develops between spouses. It's like an oasis in a desert. It doesn't have to be long, expensive, or ornate. The fact that you do it, and it's for her, says it all.

7. Invest Time in Her Interests.

Notice—I did not say invest interest in her interests, but time. It's naive to think a husband can become keenly interested in knitting, crocheting, baking, or feminine arts and crafts! But, husbands, you can invest some of your time in her interests and she in yours. Aren't we exhorted about this?

Each of you should look not only to your own interests, but also to the interests of others (Philippians 2:4).

What does your wife really enjoy doing? Take some time and do it with her. Now I know that you know—that she knows—that we all know that you don't particularly enjoy the activity; but the fact that you're willing to invest a little time doing it with her makes all the difference in the world. It confirms in her heart that your priorities are in place.

Not all cracks and breaks are repaired in marriages. Fortunately, Kevin and Marcy turned a corner. We sat down and redrew Kevin's priority list to reflect what the Scriptures really teach. Oh, there were a few lapses of memory, but eventually Kevin caught on to a new priority list. Marcy patiently worked with him in the rearrangement. Now they have a happy, fulfilled marriage. If you were to ask them today what is first in their lives, they would both say, "the Lord." Because He is first, they are now able, with His power, to focus much better on one another.

So, here are the tools needed if your marriage is not functioning properly because of disarranged priorities:

1. One eraser to erase from the board the old list.

2. One piece of chalk to write the new list.

Try it. You'll be surprised. It works. It has to. That's how the original Manufacturer wrote the directions.

Questions for Discussion

1. Who is apt to get their priorities confused most often in a marriage, the man or the woman? Why?

2. Why do you think, as a rule, it's true that "a man's life is his job while a woman's life is her family and home"?

3. Reread Matthew 6:33. How would you apply that in a Christian marriage? How does "Do unto others as you would have them do unto you" apply in a marriage?

4. What keeps a husband from placing his wife high on his priority list?

5. What is the difference between a husband being conscientious in his job and being a workaholic? Discuss the difference. What are some warning signs of a workaholic?

Project

Husbands: Over the next month, share with your wife a rough copy of your weekly schedule, with quality time scheduled in for her.

Make plans and *set a date* for a week-end getaway within the next two months.

THREE

RECLAIMING THE LOVE

Dan and Becky met in high school. After a stormy engagement period their first year of college, they were married. Dan was a bundle of energy, Becky was more "laid back," less aggressive. From all appearances, they were "madly" in love. The early years of their marriage appeared to suggest that theirs was the ideal marriage. Two children graced their home, precious little girls. They were in their thirteenth year of marriage when they made an appointment to see me. As they sat across from my desk, it was apparent they were not the same couple that went "riding off into the sunset" thirteen years ago. Physically, Dan was thirty-five pounds heavier. Though slim, Becky looked more like a person over forty than she did her actual age of thirty-two.

She spoke first, "I guess I'll start. Our problem is really not a complicated one. We just don't feel anything for each other any more . . . our love is all gone."

There was about fifteen seconds of silence that felt like thirty minutes! After looking down at the floor for a long time, finally, Dan spoke, "Well, at least Becky and I agree on this one thing. We really don't have any feeling for each other any more, and we just don't know how to gracefully end the marriage . . . I guess that's why we're here."

No financial problems, no sexual problems, no children problems, no in-law problems—it would have been easier had they been fighting. Neither had fallen for anyone else. They were "tired of pretending."

Dan and Becky had been active in the church. They attended faithfully and were consistent in their giving and participation. Dan had an above-average income; Becky was frugal. They lived in an above average home for their young age. So where do we begin? I took a deep breath, paused, then caught one word they kept using over and over again, "FEELING."

Though the solution to their dilemma would be a long road, it was not a complicated solution. In fact, it was very clear. They had a reclamation job to do in the "love department." Their biggest error from the beginning was never fully understanding what marital love really is and relying on their feelings.

It's hard to pinpoint what God has in mind in the way of marital love when we use the word "love" so loosely in our society. We say, "I love ice cream, apple pie, mountains, furs, my country, Aunt Margaret, my brother and sister, my parents, my kids, and my spouse!" All of that with the same word, LOVE.

The Greeks used different words to describe different kinds of love. For example, *phile* meant a "brotherly" or "sisterly" affection. *Eros* meant sexual love. From that we get the word, "erotic." *Storge* meant a national love, or a love for a system of thought, like a particular philosophy. Then there is *agape,* the highest kind of love you can have for another. It is agape love with which "God so loved the world."

Interestingly enough, in Ephesians 5:25 where Paul bids husbands to "love" their wives like Christ loved the church, he uses the word "agape."

Let's see if we can adequately define and explain that kind of love. Agape love is unselfish, intelligent goodwill that is both unconditional and nondemanding. It doesn't love because of the attractiveness of the object, nor because the object will do something good back to the lover. It loves without the idea of receiving something in return. It is a nonnegotiating kind of love. It doesn't strike bargains with its object. It never says, "You scratch my back and I'll scratch yours." It expects nothing in return. It sings one song, and that song is giving. It makes no demands, no threats, and puts no conditions on its object. It never manipulates or intimidates, but always has one and only one motive—to serve.

J. B. Phillips has caught the essence of love when he translates part of 1 Corinthians 13.

> This love of which I speak is slow to lose patience—it looks for a way of being constructive. It is not possessive: It is neither anxious to impress, nor does it cherish inflated ideas of its own importance. Love has good manners and does not pursue selfish advantage. It is not touchy. It does not keep account of evil or gloat over the wickedness of other people. On the contrary, it is glad with all men when truth prevails. Love knows no limit to its endurance, no end to its trust, no fading of its hope; it can outlast anything. It is in fact the one thing that still stands when all else has fallen (1 Corinthians 13:4-8).

Wow! What a description! It would take us months just to discover the impact of only a few of those words. One thing for sure . . . agape love, the kind married people are to have for each other, is more than just a euphoric feeling or wistful nostalgia. It's more than just the arousal of the physical glands or a temporary swelling emotion. It can be summed up in one word—COMMITMENT. It is not commitment based on the worthiness of the object, or commitment based on the guarantee of mutual commitment. It is unqualified, unconditional, unrestricted commitment.

Feelings come and go. Arousals are temporary. Physical attractiveness changes. Not even the "fountain of youth" in St. Augustine, Florida can immunize you from the fact that you will look different at 55 that you did at 25. Most of us have the same things we had thirty years earlier—they have just shifted!

Dan and Becky had been physically attracted to each other in their youth. They fell in what they thought was "love," but in reality, it was little more than highly charged emotional feelings (passion). There was very little commitment involved in their relationship. Just feelings! And when the feelings went, so did what they thought was love.

Our commitment to our spouse is one that is physical, mental, emotional, sexual, and practical. It is commitment regardless of what the outer circumstances may do. It is commitment regardless of the cost or the inconvenience.

What about the couple who marries, and only eighteen months into the marriage, he is injured in the pelvic area leaving him unable to have sex for the rest of his life? Does she just "dump" him because he can no longer bring her pleasure? Do you spell her love c-o-m-m-i-t-m-e-n-t? Should she stay committed to him until death?

Or what about the strong marriage suddenly interrupted by the wife having a stroke. Does she all of a sudden become a liability where before she was once an asset? Marriage is first of all a relationship between two people based on a mutual commitment. Long after the titillating feelings are gone, long after the euphoria has disappeared, long after the bells and whistles have ceased, the commitment is still there.

Needed Steps to Reclaim the Love

If you "feel" your love for your spouse is gone, what do you do? Do you just "throw in the proverbial towel"? NO! You take the needed steps to regain and reclaim the love. What are those steps?

Step One: Recognize before God that you misunderstood what Biblical marital love really is.

This is not an easy acknowledgement, especially if you've been married for a long time. This step is extremely essential before anything constructive can take place. It is, in a sense, a confession. It is a "coming clean" before God that you, not your spouse, have been on the wrong track of love. A simple prayer like this will do

> Dear God, I confess to you that I've misunderstood what real agape love is. I have bought into the world's system and its definition of love, but I openly confess the wrongness of that faulty definition. I acknowledge to you that real marital love first and foremost involves commitment to my spouse, REGARDLESS of my feelings and emotions.
>
> I recognize that the right kind of love is unconditional commitment, regardless of how much or how many times my spouse has changed. Amen.

Sound simple? In one respect it is; yet from another perspective, we have a difficult time with a prayer like that because it is an acknowledgement of failure. It's somewhat like the little boy who kept hitting his sister and saying, "You're so stupid." Finally his mother intervened, saying, "Johnny, tell your sister you're sorry." He resisted. His mother threatened to spank him; so finally in desperation, he turned to his sister and said, "I'M SORRY YOU'RE SO STUPID!" It's tough to admit we've been wrong.

Step Two: Believe that God has the ability to give you the true love needed for your spouse.

We say with our lips that we believe God can do anything; but when it comes to our marriage, we wince at that statement. In a sense, every divorce is an admission on the part of one or both of the spouses that there is one area where God is not all-powerful. It's almost like saying, "God, I know you can part the Red Sea, you can rescue Daniel miraculously from the lion's mouth, you can walk on water, you can raise your Son from the dead; but the one thing you are unable to do is restore my love for my spouse." Now, no one would ever dream of saying that, but in essence that's exactly what we say when we give up and "throw in the towel."

God had to remind Jeremiah.

> Then the word of the Lord came to Jeremiah: I am the Lord, the God of all mankind. Is anything too hard for me? (Jeremiah 32:26-27).

Essential to reclaiming your love for your spouse is to recognize that you can't do it on you own; it will take the intervening hand of God. Guess what? He's waiting, ready, and anxious to intervene for you!

Step Three: Begin to demonstrate in visible acts agape love for your spouse.

Oh, how we can resist that, especially when we don't have any "feelings" for that person? Learn this: feelings follow facts, not the other way around. In the outward demonstration of love, you are confirming the reality of the inward love. Most people say, "Well, when the feelings return, I'll do the demonstrating." No, it's just the opposite. We need to do the demonstrating SO THAT the feelings will return. Love is a hollow, gushy, mushy, ethereal "mishmash" unless the deeds are present. Scripture tells us,

> Dear children, let us not love with words or tongue but with actions and in truth (1 John 3:18).

**Step Four: Don't monitor and evaluate how your demon-
stration of love to your spouse is working.**

Remember, true agape love expects nothing in return. I've
discovered if you expect nothing in return, when nothing
comes back, you're not disappointed. But when something
does come back, it's like icing on the cake. Remember, it's
your responsibility to love; it's God's responsibility to work
in and through that love to change your spouse's attitude toward you.

I remember a woman coming to me once and praying,
"Lord you love my husband, and I'll change him." Wrong
prayer! It should have been, "I'll love him, Lord. You change
him." God has never commissioned any spouse to be a "change
agent" for the other. Our responsibility is to love, and if
you're a man reading this, you are to love as Christ loved the
church. Leave it, or allow God to do the necessary changing.

Step Five: Begin a prayer "conspiracy" for your spouse!

Sound devious? It really isn't. In fact, it's quite Biblical.
We are told to pray for one another "that you may be healed"
(James 5:16). Don't just pray, "God help my spouse to treat
me decently." That is a tad selfish. Instead, ask God to bless
your spouse, to make his or her way prosperous, and to con-
vict him/her in areas where that is needed. Be specific. But remember to keep the selfish requests out of it. The Bible clearly
teaches that we are not to pray selfishly.

> When you ask, you do not receive, because you ask with
> wrong motives, that you may spend what you get on your
> pleasures (James 4:3).

How might such a prayer go? Without putting words in
your mouth, an effective prayer may go like this:

Dear God, I bring to you today _____. I call your power to bear upon his (her) life just now. Bless him (her) with your goodness, your direction, your abundance. Lord, I love _____ and pray that his (her) welfare and good may be remembered by you. Lord, encourage, inspire, uplift, and sanctify him (her). Give me the opportunity today to demonstrate my love to him (her). Amen.

It isn't that prayer changes things, but when we pray for others, God changes them. (God may even change the pray-er!) This is never truer than in marriage.

Step Six: Resist with authority all temptations to be interested in anyone else.

There is a myth that rears its ugly head again and again in marriage that says, "If I have strong feelings for someone besides my wife, it must be good evidence that I'm to be with her, and that my marriage is wrong." Perish the thought!! Again, feelings have come to deceive even the strongest among us. People who "feel" they've lost their love for their mate begin redirecting their emotions (and eyes) to others to see what else is "out there." Nothing could be more deceiving and disastrous.

Maybe you're saying right now, "But I don't want to have my love restored for my spouse because I'm interested in someone else." Friend, it's not a matter of what you want or how you feel! What really matters is what God's Word says. If you are married, you entered into a covenant relationship with God and your spouse. That covenant cannot and should not be broken. Maybe your line of reasoning is that your spouse doesn't want to restore the love either. Again, I repeat, it doesn't matter what they want or feel. What really counts is what God's Word says. Since marriage is a three-way covenant, it only takes two standing for a marriage for it to win—you and

God. Malachi 2:15-16 speaks of that covenant, then God adds, "I hate divorce."

During the process of reclaiming your love, resist even the thought of anyone else. Don't even look at anyone else. Above all, don't try to be with anyone else. It only "muddies the waters."

Step Seven: Ask your spouse to verbally identify those areas of your life that are detrimental for a love relationship.

This is humbling. But in the practice of this kind of humility, God does a number on the heart of your spouse. It starts by assuring them that you are willing to go to any length or depth for agape love to bloom and blossom in your relationship. Again, don't base this on feeling, but on the clear command of Scripture that says:

> Humble yourselves before the Lord and He will lift you up (James 4:10).

The highest a man ever stands is when he is on his knees inviting his peers to identify his areas of weakness and inadequacy so he can do something about them.

Step Eight: Learn to say many times daily "I love you," even when you don't feel love.

When you say "I love you," you're really saying "I'm committed to you." Since agape love is unconditional commitment, you can, with all honesty, say those words and mean them.

What if your spouse doesn't say them back? That is not your problem or concern. Remember, God has not called you to monitor your spouse's response. He is holding you responsible for what you're supposed to do. Do it.

One more truth must be stated before closing this section. Guess who stole the love away that you had for your spouse? You guessed it, the devil. Remember:

The thief comes only to steal and kill and destroy (John 10:10).

This is especially true in marriage. I believe that Satan desires first and foremost to damage and destroy marriage because it is God's oldest institution and the most powerful. When you stop and think, all of the ills of our society today — abortion, homosexuality, drugs, pornography, and suicide — could all be eliminated if all the marriages in our country were what God planned for them to be.

Remember, your lost love can be reclaimed. God will do it, but only through you. What about it?

Questions for Discussion

1. Write down five synonyms for love on a piece of paper. If you're a male, write "M" at the top of the sheet but not your name. If female, write "F" at the top of the sheet without your name. Fold the paper in two and have a moderator read them, making a cumulative list of male and female suggestions. What are the differences in the two lists? Why? Does this suggest that men and women view the concept of love differently?

2. What role does "feeling" play in love? Why can marital love never be confined to just good feelings for each other?

3. If true agape love is commitment of one to another, can love be restored in a marriage by each partner making that commitment, then following through with visible acts of love?

4. Have everyone in the group write their own definition of unconditional love. Read all the definitions aloud. Why is this so hard to apply to marriage?

Project

For couples: Without identifying what they are, let each spouse do two or three acts of love this week other than the sex act. At the end of the week, discuss the effect of these acts.

REPAIRING THE HURT

Debbie looked as if she were despairing of life itself. She was ashamed to tell her story, not ashamed of herself, but ashamed for anyone to think she would still stay with her husband after what he had revealed. They had not yet celebrated their tenth anniversary; and from what she shared, I had serious doubts they would. She had no reason to ever suspect Tom of any marital unfaithfulness. He had been a good provider, a responsive father to their two children. Although they hadn't spent a lot of time together as husband and wife because of his job, unfaithfulness was the last thought to ever enter her head. Then it happened like a bombshell.

She picked him up at the airport as usual. He always traveled during the third week of every month. In unpacking his suitcase, a small card fell out of his shirt pocket which read, "Thanks for the unforgettable evening and gift. I'll cherish our moments together. Love, Diane." She broke out in a cold sweat at first. Then gathering her thoughts, hoping against hope, mused to herself, "He's playing a joke on me."

Unfortunately, it was no joke. When confronted with the card, Tom caved in and began to weep. He admitted to an affair that had been in progress for the better part of a year.

Debbie told me she felt violated, betrayed, cheap. But above all, extremely hurt. She felt herself to be a total failure as a wife. Tom pleaded for forgiveness, and demonstrated an agonizing repentance. Debbie's response now for three weeks had been one of total indifference. The emotion was not anger, revenge, or hatred—just a severe hurt which, in her words, was worse than any physical pain she had ever endured, including the pain of bearing her two children without benefit of anesthetic! Her face and voice manifested her feelings.

Prematurely, most of us would say that Debbie had Biblical grounds for divorce and should immediately begin proceedings for such. But Tom and Debbie were both professing Christians. And while technically and Biblically she had a right to divorce him, she knew deep down that she was under a higher principle in Scripture, and that was, "forgiving each other, just as in Christ God forgave you" (Ephesians 4:32).

How many have sighed, "Oh, if that just weren't in the Bible." But it is.

Tom and Debbie's scenario did end in forgiveness. But the hurt was still there, the damage was done, and now the real question was, "How is the hurt repaired?" No marriage repair kit should ever be without a "hurt healer-upper."

Adultery isn't the only thing that brings hurt to a marriage. Distrust, unkind and harsh words, built-up resentment, and avoidance can also bring hurt.

Hurts come in all shapes and sizes. They come in all degrees of devastation. Hurts occur when one spouse basically ignores the other; hurts come when a spouse belittles and puts down the other; hurts occur when a spouse has been taken advantage of, is lied to, or is taken for granted. Many hurts come when a wife, for example, feels she no longer is a viable part of the marriage relationship—that somehow she doesn't matter, doesn't count, or isn't germane to the family anymore other than as a dishwasher and laundry lady.

So the question is, how is the hurt repaired? Effective repair comes when we remember a series of truths that never change. Let's examine them one by one.

1. Remember, Most Hurts Come from Carelessness, and Are Not Inflicted on Purpose.

Now obviously, in Tom's case, it wasn't a matter of carelessness, but a matter of outright sin. But much hurt is inflicted from not thinking through our words and actions. Failure to call when you're late, forgetting to send a birthday card, overlooking Valentine's Day . . . all of these fall into the category of just plain carelessness on the part of one spouse. Accept them that way. And forgive!

2. Healing of Hurts Is Hastened When the Offender Is Blessed!

Now, I know that sounds totally illogical. Yet Jesus taught us,

> Blessed are you when men hate you, when they exclude you and insult you and reject your name as evil, because of the Son of Man (Luke 6:22).

There is a tremendous power when we return blessing for reviling or hurt. Of course, our first impulse and carnal urge is to strike back, to demonstrate some kind of vengeance. Don't forget, vengeance is His, not ours.

3. Remember to Hand Your Hurts over to the Lord!

The Devil wants to harass us by encouraging us to harbor our hurts and nurse them. The Bible is clear in what we're to do with our cares: "Cast your cares on the Lord and he will sustain you; he will never let the righteous fall" (Psalm 55:22).

And what about Peter's admonition as translated by J. B. Phillips?

> You can throw the whole weight of your anxieties upon him for you are his personal concern (1 Peter 5:7).

Remember, there are some things God never intended that we carry on our shoulders; hurt is one of those things.

4. Remember, Hurt Is Temporary, Never Permanent!

I love the Psalms. In fact, no marriage repair kit would be complete without a copy of that great wisdom and devotional literature included.

Listen to what David shared from personal experience: "Weeping may remain for a night, but rejoicing comes in the morning" (Psalm 30:5).

That's God's way of saying, HURT ISN'T PERMANENT. It does pass. It's not that "time heals all wounds." Time heals nothing, but God does in time.

5. Remember, Hurts Are Deepened by Retaliation.

There is something in all of us that always wants to retaliate when we've been hurt. We want to "get back" by some form of revenge. A man recently said to me, "I was so hurt by the supervisor's decision. I've been plotting all week how I'm going to get him to pay through the nose over that decision." Not only is that kind of thinking nonproductive, it is destructive, and only serves to drive the hurt deeper. Like a boomerang, it comes right back to us, and often with momentum.

Vengeance is destructive, of all places, in marriage. When you have been wronged by your spouse, it becomes doubly wrong to wrong them back. Guess who suffers most from such action? You got it—you. Here, as no other place, we need to hear again the warning:

> Do not repay anyone evil for evil. Be careful to do what is right in the eyes of everybody. If it is possible, as far as it depends on you, live at peace with everyone. Do not take revenge, my friends, but leave room for God's wrath, for it is written: 'It is mine to avenge; I will repay,' says the Lord (Romans 12:17-19).

Humanly speaking, it seems reasonable that we can express some holy and righteous indignation when we are wronged to the point of hurt. But it only "muddies the water." When we try to do what God alone is capable of doing perfectly, we only botch up the whole episode. It's as if God is saying to you, "You let me handle the revenge department; I know how and when to do it right."

6. Remember, Don't Wallow in Self-Pity When You're Hurt!

Self-pity is an attitude we naturally lean toward when we've been severely hurt. No one else pities us, so we take it on ourselves to do the pitying. That attitude turns us into a person few people really want to be around. It makes us most miserable, those about us miserable, and renders us temporarily incapable of functioning. Self-pity is one of the most selfish attitudes anyone can acquire. It serves only to feed and perpetuate the hurt, making us dwell upon it.

7. Remember, Let the Offender Know, in the Spirit of Love, That God Is Using the Hurt.

I have always been thoroughly enamored with the account of Joseph and his brothers in Genesis. What they did to him was not only inhumane, it went against everything they had been taught as small boys. Their actions landed Joseph in Egypt where more than once he almost lost his life. On one occasion he almost lost his high standard of purity by being placed in a vulnerable position. But he persevered. When his brothers came to Egypt to get food for survival, little did they know that Joseph had been elevated to Pharaoh's right-hand man. It was well within Joseph's power to refuse his brothers in retaliation. However, Joseph knew something his brothers never learned. God uses unjust things and even hurts to accomplish His larger purpose.

I've always been excited over Joseph's explanation to his brothers.

> You intended to harm me, but God intended it for good to accomplish what is now being done, the saving of many lives (Genesis 50:20).

What a spirit! If that spirit prevailed in marriages in response to hurt, it would transform sour marriages into matrimonial victories.

Well, there is one more piece of instruction on how to repair the hurts that come in marriage.

8. Remember, There Is Healing in Forgiveness.

We Christians often play games with the whole arena of forgiveness. I heard a speaker say once, "It's a neat thing to forgive." No, it's not just a "neat" thing to forgive; it is an obligatory thing for the believer to forgive. Jesus made that clear:

> For if you forgive men when they sin against you, your heavenly Father will also forgive you. But if you do not forgive men their sins, your Father will not forgive your sins (Matthew 6:14-15).

That is strong language. Jesus made it plain that forgiveness isn't optional for the believer. If we've been forgiven by God, who do we think we are that we are qualified to withhold forgiveness from others that have wronged us, ESPECIALLY OUR SPOUSES. The miracle of forgiveness, however, isn't just what it does for the offender. The real blessing comes in what it does for the forgiver.

The good news is that hurts can be repaired. But it's really up to us.

Even though Debbie extended her forgiveness to Tom, the residue of that hurt lingered. By her own testimony much later, it finally was lifted because she prayed daily for her spouse and herself that God would somehow increase her love for her husband. It worked. And . . . it will work for you. Hurts need never be final. God will always heal them when our hearts are willing and open to His Will.

If you feel that it is necessary, here's a good prayer for you to pray verbatim every day for the next two weeks if you have been hurt by your spouse.

Dear God, I've been hurt by _____. God, I know you have forgiven _____, so now I forgive _____ too. I pray for you to mightily bless _____ and make _____ way prosper. Lord, I lift my hurt to You and ask You to receive it. Help me never to take it back again. Amen!

However, it might even be better to use your own prayer if these words really don't fit you. You don't need to fit someone else's mold!

Questions for Discussion

1. Do you agree or disagree with this statement: The "mandate" to forgive takes precedent over the "right" to divorce in cases of marital unfaithfulness? (Cf. Ephesians 5:32) Why or why not?

2. Should we seek to "bless" our spouse when they hurt us even if we don't "feel" good about blessing them? What are some ways we can practically bless them?

3. Why do you think revenge or retaliation is limited to God and not given to us? Why do you think our retaliation only worsens our relationship to our mate?

4. Why do you think it is so difficult to hand our hurts over to the Lord? What did Jesus do when offended? (Cf. 1 Peter 2:23)

Project

Do this personally and privately when no one is around. Make a list on paper of the hurts inflicted on you by your spouse. Include everything in this list, even what you consider to be minor hurts. Get a tinfoil pan, place your list in the pan, then strike a match to it. While it burns, read 1 Peter 5:7 and pray this prayer aloud:

> God, I lift to you all these hurts and anxieties that I feel (*your mate*) has inflicted on me. Bless (*your mate*) and show me how I too can bless him/her.
>
> Amen.

FIVE

REMAKING THE RUTS

A hand-painted sign was seen tacked to a board and stuck in the dirt: "CHOOSE YOUR RUTS CAREFULLY, YOU'LL BE IN THEM FOR THE NEXT 7 MILES." That sign placed at the beginning of a dirt road in east Tennessee reminds us of warning signs given to couples as they begin their lives together.

No matter how much you fight it, a routineness sets in to marriage that is similar to ruts. Couples do certain things at certain times in certain ways for certain reasons. All of a sudden before they know it, they are living a rutted existence. A wearisome boredom sets in to many marriages and lasts for years sometimes before couples have the courage to break out, to plow new ground, and if nothing more, to make some new ruts where there have been none.

Many things contribute to a "rutted" marriage. Most of them are so subtle that couples aren't even aware they're present until the ruts are so deep the "axle is scraping." What are these culprits?

Dreams Gone Stale

Most marriages begin with colorful dreams about the future. Vocation goals are discussed; the coming of children is talked about with excitement; that "dream home" is pictured and "drooled over." But the daily grind of work, paying pressing bills, keeping the car running, the rent paid, maintaining contact with two families—all contribute to the same ruts on the same days, and the dreams about the future go by the board. I've counseled couples for years to set aside some quality time weekly, even if they must put it on their calendars, to do nothing but talk about their dreams and plans for the future, taking some time to commit those dreams to God. That way, routines are broken, new ground is plowed, and ruts don't have an opportunity to form.

Lack of New Friends

Most couples make this error. No new friendships are developed, so a staleness sets in. Then you have another set of ruts almost cast in concrete. It's good to have old reliable friends with whom you maintain close contact—people that you can really count on when you need a helping hand, some advice, or just close fellowship. But in the process, don't forget to be consistently making new friends, or your ruts will be so deep and set, it will be very hard to turn your wheels out of them.

Financial Worries

Keeping the world away from the door is one thing. Creating one financial crisis after another because of indiscriminate and irresponsible spending is another. Couples can become so bogged down in battling the problem of "too much month left over at the end of the money," they find it almost impossible to break out of this rut.

Work Addiction

This rut can ruin a good marriage. It is usually created by the husband, but wives are not exempt! It most often occurs when both partners are working outside the home. There aren't enough hours in the working day to do the task, so work is brought home. If the work isn't brought home, the weariness is. Young husbands, anxious to please their bosses while working their way up the corporate ladder, are often found staying over till 5:30, 6:00, 6:30, or even 7:00 P.M. Or worse, they bring their briefcase home full of work, which means they have robbed their wives of precious time while home. Of course, occasionally this is necessary and not harmful; but it's when it becomes habitual that a rut is built that is hard to "reroute."

Often, couples find that the topic of their conversation at home is work, work, work. Often their conversation degenerates down to their frustrations at work.

This rut needs to be remade by leaving your work at the office, or the shop, or the classroom. It is so essential where both partners work and are away from each other for nine hours per day to devote their conversation to positive, constructive topics when at home together. If not careful, couples can build their whole relationship around all the ramifications of their jobs. If you can identify with this, it's time to get the sledge hammer out and bust this rut right now.

In-Law Bondage

Another rut that can develop easily in couples' lives is too much time spent with in-laws. In-laws are wonderful people. Let me remind you that when you married your spouse, in a sense, you married his/her parents as well. And rightly so, because he or she is a product of those parents. Your spouse doesn't exist in a vacuum. Proper time and attention needs to be paid to parents of both sides. Certainly holidays like Christmas, Easter, and Thanksgiving (along with birthdays and anniversaries) are great times for the extended families to be together.

But the rut I'm speaking of here is deeper than that. It is an inordinate obsession to be constantly with in-laws, eating many meals there, spending many evenings and all week-ends there. This rut robs couples of time that is much needed for them to spend alone. It also has a tendency to "wear out the welcome" regardless of how close you may be to your parents. Inordinate visitation is not a healthy thing.

And, by the way . . . if you're one of those in-laws, if you have married children, don't feel you have to visit them daily, or even weekly. You can be guilty of building a rut that is very difficult to break out of later. This is something couples ought to discuss before marriage, and even after marriage.

Television Addiction

I just read where the average American home today has the television set on forty-nine and one-half hours weekly. The average five-year-old spends 25 hours per week in front of the tube. Often, because of a tight budget, couples will opt to stay home and turn on the tube . . . watching it for as long as six or seven hours at a time in one evening. A slight diversion from this today, of course, is the option of renting a movie. But even that can become addictive, so that much of your waking hours together consist of four eyes watching the tube for extended periods of time. Again, this is very unhealthy not to mention a poor use of time.

Of course, there is nothing unhealthy about sitting down together occasionally to watch a movie, a T.V. special, or a sports event. But indiscriminate T.V. viewing can become a very poor substitute for healthy communication. One couple I know broke this rut by declaring Monday, Wednesday, and Thursday nights as off-limits for the T.V. It's turned off on those nights and this couple finds a different diversion. No one will check this for you; you must take the initiative and do it yourself.

Also, remember that in the past ten years, practically all censorship has been removed from network programming.

This means that occurrences of violence, illicit sex, perversion, and sadism are on the increase at an unprecedented rate. So continual, unrestrained watching can bring some real emotional damage to your marital relationship. Thus, don't allow this rut to afflict your marriage. It will if left unchecked.

Literary Rut

In this age of fast foods, slow digestion, and quick staccato information, it is easy for couples to ignore any kind of reading. You can't depend on videos for everything. How long has it been since you and your spouse read a good book together and discussed its content? This is not a generation of readers. It's easier to listen to a tape or watch a video or even attend a seminar. All married couples should make it a goal to read at least four good books a year and discuss those books. This will nudge you out of your comfort zone and stimulate you in areas where you need to be stretched. There are some excellent books out on marriage, home, the family, discipleship, Christian growth, the church, the Holy Spirit, and endtime prophecy. An occasional novel or biography is good, stimulating reading and provides great conversation material.

Some couples haven't read a book in five years. Maybe you're one who says, "But I don't like to read, and it takes me forever to finish a book." That's all right, take as long as you like, but read. It will eventually get you off of dead center and keep you from becoming stale.

The Financial Rut

Because more will be said later on this big topic, suffice it to say only one thing now: this can be a disastrous rut. In an age of easy credit, some couples fall into the "plastic money" rut where they pay for everything with the card. Bad habit, bad habit. The day of reckoning comes.

Others succumb to "spontaneous spending." This is a habit where you go shopping, not for something specific, but for whatever grabs your fancy. You always end up buying what you don't need or can't afford with this rut.

Staying overdrawn in your checkbook because your standard of living is a tad higher than your income is truly a rut that leads to ruin. Break it before it breaks you. Every couple can throw their budget to the wind, but they will surely reap the whirlwind. If you're in the rut of irresponsible financial spending, get out while there's time. These ruts have a way of hardening quicker than all the rest.

These and more ruts can devastate marriages and must be broken, not just once, but again and again. Remember, it's your responsibility to keep your marriage fresh, stimulating, new, and exciting. Don't allow any rut to bury you.

Questions for Discussion

1. What is the most obvious "culprit" that bring ruts into a marriage? Why?

2. What do you feel are the most dangerous and destructive ruts in a marriage? Why are they worse than others?

3. How can you bring some variation and creativity to even the most routine things? (Be creative for a few minutes and think!)

Project

Monday, Day 1: Sleep on the opposite side of the bed from where you normally sleep.

Tuesday, Day 2: Let none of your conversation be in the area of your work unless absolutely necessary.

Wednesday, Day 3: Get up 15 minutes earlier today and read Ephesians 5 together.

Thursday, Day 4: Have someone over for dessert you've never had before.

Friday, Day 5: Leave the T.V. off this evening for the whole evening and read a chapter in a good book *together.*

Saturday, Day 6: Go visit a beauty spot or tourist attraction you've never seen.

Sunday, Day 7: Go to church early today and sit in a different section.

REMOVING
THE DEBRIS

Our old clothes dryer finally blew! After many repair jobs over the years, it finally bit the dust. After hooking our brand new dryer up, I opened the door, and out fell the Operating Instruction sheet. At the bottom of the page in bold black letters it read,

For peak efficiency, keep filter free of all lint and debris.

If a clothes dryer won't run right when there's too much debris in its works, why do we think a marriage will run smoothly when it's full of debris?

Some homes have a piece of furniture known as a "catch-all." It catches everything from car keys, pop cans, change, to the morning mail. Ours sits right in our entry way. Every two or three days, we need to "clear the debris."

Marriage, like any catch-all, needs to be cleared regularly and consistently of the debris that gathers. Some of this marital debris comes from carelessness; some, just from the routineness of being married, and some, from sheer neglect. Every marriage I know needs a good spring housecleaning about three or four times per year. There are some things we need to pitch out, or they will smother or, at best, stifle a good marriage. Left unswept, the debris will pile higher and higher until the marriage can no longer breathe. That's the prelude to a dead marriage.

What particles of debris do we need to eliminate from marriage?

Neglect

Neglect is a subtle piece of dust that slowly creeps into a marriage to jam the works. Neglect comes in all shapes and sizes. It comes in seasons. But come it will unless we take proper precautions.

Many husbands have become connoisseurs of the fine art of neglect—not intentionally, of course. As one husband put it, "It's the nature of the beast." They neglect to compliment their wife's appearance, cooking, housekeeping, sewing, driving, creativity, thriftiness—where does the list stop? Wives become so busy cooking the meals, washing the clothes, bathing the kids, balancing the checkbook, and filling the dishwasher. They, too, fall into a state of neglect from time to time. They neglect, at times, to keep their attractiveness up, to compliment their husband's abilities, skills, or the way he excels in his hobby. Both partners neglect to touch, to kiss, to speak romantic words, and basically to affirm each other.

I've found it beneficial for spouses to occasionally ask their mates, "Do you feel I've been neglecting you lately?" Busy schedules contribute to neglect. Getting caught up in projects, hobbies, or special interests can hinder focusing attention on the other. How about you, reader, are you willing to ask yourself the questions: Have I been neglecting my spouse lately? When was the last time I actually complimented him on something he did well? How long has it been since I mentioned she looked nice in a particular outfit? This piece of debris is a sneaky one, usually very "quiet," but it can do a lot of damage if left unswept.

Complaining

Some couples spell this word "n-a-g-g-i-n-g." It is often referred to as griping. It is the registering of disapproval of what the other says or does: The food is too spicy; you don't make enough money; you don't manage our money very well; you spend too much; your hair is too short; your driving is too reckless; you're gaining too much weight. On and on it goes in the complaint department.

> Sticks and stones can break my bones, but words can never hurt me.

Remember that little ditty? Oh, if it were only true. Leveling complaints consistently at our spouses has a way of wearing down love and respect.

> Reckless words pierce like a sword, but the tongue of the wise brings healing (Proverbs 12:18).

Again,

> He who guards his lips guards his soul, but he who speaks rashly will come to ruin (Proverbs 13:3).

> The tongue that brings healing is a tree of life, but a deceitful tongue crushes the spirit (Proverbs 15:4).

Jesus made it clear that by our words we are justified, and by our words we are condemned. This is one piece of debris that no marriage can afford to allow to linger. It has to go.

When Stephanie and Larry asked to see me, I couldn't imagine what they wanted. Marriage counseling was the last thing on earth I would have ever dreamed of doing with this couple. Their marriage of nearly twelve years appeared from the outside to be the epitome of marital bliss. There was, however, another story. I saw another side of this couple as they sat in my office and she began to pour out her heart, going through a whole box of tissues in the process. It was only one song, though it has many verses.

Larry had complained since the night of their honeymoon twelve years ago. He found fault with virtually everything she did, said, made, and was. She never quite "measured up." He pleaded guilty! His complaining attitude only manifested itself in his marriage. In asking what kind of home life he had grown up in, I was not surprised at his answer. Larry's dad was an overpowering man, was abusive in his speech, but was remembered because nothing his wife ever did pleasedhim. Larry had learned his complaining attitude from his father. Not until it threatened the demise of his own marriage did he fully realize the implications of such a habit.

We read together some Scripture, and I left him with the most convicting passage:

> Let your conversation be always full of grace, seasoned with salt, so that you may know how to answer everyone (Colossians 4:6).

Solomon was so right when he gave us this other warning:

> Do you see a man who speaks in haste? There is more hope for a fool than for him (Proverbs 29:20).

The dust and grime of complaining will so clog the marriage relationship that it becomes a spoiler of affections.

Quarreling

This piece of debris left unchecked can bring permanent damage that can't be repaired. Like water poured on the ground, it can't be gathered up if it is allowed to go too far.

The amount of violence in marriages has increased by 37 percent in the last five years. No longer are there just centers for battered women, but for battered men — and sadly, battered children who try to break up the fights brought on by arguments between spouses.

What brings on quarreling in marriage? Really only one thing, each spouse trying to prove to the other that he or she is right.

The Bible is pretty forthright in this area.

A quarrelsome wife is like a constant dripping on a rainy day; restraining her is like restraining the wind or grasping oil with the hand (Proverbs 27:15-16).

Again,

Better to live in a desert than with a quarrelsome and ill-tempered wife (Proverbs 21:19).

Better to live on a corner of the roof than share a house with a quarrelsome wife (Proverbs 21:9).

What more shall I say? If you're a man reading this and thinking that you're off the hook, think again. What is good for the goose is good for the gander! Implied in those verses is that it's just as wrong for a husband to be quarrelsome. Verbal assault in marriage not only has no place, it is totally non-productive and can lead quickly to fatality.

When you stop and think, it always takes two people to have an argument. If just one spouse will keep his mouth shut, that ends the argument right there.

I challenge you to try this experiment. The next time you are pulled into a volley of words with your spouse, just don't respond — except with words of love and affirmation. It will end the argument before it ever gets started.

The poet was so right when he said,

How like an arrow is a word
At random often speeding;
To find a target never meant
And set some heart a bleeding.
O pray that Heaven may seal the lips
Ere unkind words are spoken
For Heaven itself cannot recall
When once that seal is broken.

It's no wonder James says that we need to be quick to hear and slow to speak. Verbal assassination in marriage can be the most destructive piece of debris to clean up that there is.

Suspicion

The "machine" of marriage will not run long if this culprit comes to stay. Suspicion is a product of distrust. It eats like a cancer at the one being suspicious while destroying something very precious in the one over whom the suspicion is cast.

Suspicion is not just suspecting one's spouse is interested in another person. It spills over into the areas of money, pleasure, and hobbies.

Jerry told me of his haunting suspicions of his wife. He constantly suspected that she was squandering money, secretly buying things they didn't need—things for herself and things for the house. He almost daily examined the checkbook stubs; he went through her change purse, counting her money; he searched the house looking for items she might have bought and concealed from him. It was eating him alive.

I suggested he confess his suspicions to his wife, clear the air, and see if indeed he had a right to be suspicious. The whole episode turned around on him. It turned out she was secretly stashing a little away that was unaccounted for, but it was to buy him a bench saw he had wanted for two years. Did he ever eat humble pie, and it was all over his face! He discovered that not only were his suspicions totally unfounded, but that they had really clogged their marriage, damaging their relationship with each other. Fortunately his wife had a sense of humor, forgave him, and laughed it off. But it taught him a great lesson that suspicion can cause real damage.

Suspicion has a way of building. The suspicious person adds worry to worry, and ends up making a federal case over something no larger than an ant hill! Suspicion is born of worry that is unnecessary. Some wise person wrote this:

> Some of your hurts you have cured,
> And the sharpest you still have survived,
> But what torments of grief you've endured,
> From the evils that never arrived!

There is only one way you can get rid of suspicions in marriage. COMMUNICATION! The time to strike is when the first suspicion comes. A good approach might be like this:

> Honey, I know this probably sounds dumb, but I've let my imagination run wild, and I want to confess I've had suspicions about _____. I guess I just needed to get this off my chest and let you tell me how wrong those suspicions are.

You can't go wrong with an approach like that.

Bullheadedness

The sophisticated word for this, of course, is stubbornness. This piece of debris can create a stand-off in a marriage that can go on and on, wearing both partners out in the process. Being bullheaded is digging your feet in, holding unswervingly to your position, not budging or backing off one bit. But when two people do this, there is usually a terrible crash and clash. There is a physical law in our universe that goes like this, "Two immovable pieces of material cannot occupy the same place at the same time."

I have been told by Boeing engineers that the Jumbo 747 jetliner has great elasticity in its wing span. I was told the wings are engineered and built to have a flexibility of fifteen feet up and down at the tip of each wing. That is built in so that when they hit terrific turbulence, the plane can "roll" with the storm and won't fall apart in mid-air. I'm glad they thought of that little item, aren't you?

By the same token, spouses need to build into their marriage that same flexibility. You will hit some storms, and some of them will be rough. Without the resiliency of flexibility and humility, a marriage won't survive when it hits the storm. This is especially true when both spouses are taking a rigid stand, refusing to budge and give. This kind of flexibility is called "mutual submission," and is a *must* if a marriage is to survive. We tend to forget that in the marriage section of Ephesians following the command to be filled with the Holy Spirit, Paul says, "Submit to one another out of reverence for Christ" (Ephesians 5:21).

This is why I counsel every couple considering marriage that they dare not come into marriage with a focus on their "rights." I have never known a marriage to survive on rights. It is, however, the forfeiture of rights that brings a harmony to marriage.

We belong to a culture that has convinced many men that it's less than masculine to give in. Men have bought into a mythical notion that because God has made them the head of the marriage, they have an image to maintain, and giving in or acquiescing is detrimental to that image. Nothing could be farther from God's plan.

Somehow, I believe Paul must have had marriage in mind when he said,

Do nothing out of selfish ambition or vain conceit, but in humility, consider others better than yourselves (Philippians 2:3).

If that command is obeyed, the debris of bullheadedness will disappear out of marriage. It's no fun butting heads all the time! All you get from that is one big headache. Holy wedlock becomes an "unholy deadlock," and soon the joy is gone from the marriage.

As you read these words, will you examine your own attitude toward your spouse. Are you bullheaded because you fear if you're not and don't stand up for your rights, you'll lose the controlling edge over your marriage? Forget it! And guess what! Giving in more and more does a number on your spouse, softening the heart and causing a mutual giving in. Try it, you'll be surprised.

Exhaustion

When the repairman finally stood up after having his head in the working parts of our dishwasher, he smiled and said, "I found the problem! Your dishwasher is exhausted from constant use with no rest, it's worn out!" Before I said, "How could it be?" I remembered that it was the original one that came when the house was new—18 years ago! If I had gone at the pace it had, endured the heat and the friction of the working parts for that many years, I would be worn out, too.

No marriage can survive long if exhaustion sets in with no relief. It is indeed a culprit that immobilizes and paralyzes wedded bliss. The average mother serves as a housecleaner, laundry woman, chauffeur, cook, accountant, sex-partner, seamstress, painter, nurse, and romancer. The average husband and father is expending energy daily with the pressures of being the provider, running a three-ring circus at the office, fighting traffic, and trying to respond to all the people vying for his attention. Seek solutions to the exhaustion problem *before* you are too exhausted to do something about it.

Questions for Discussion

1. Why do you think couples tend to neglect each other after a very few years of marriage? Does routineness breed neglect?

2. Is it possible for griping and complaining in marriage to be done without the complainer realizing it?

3. At what point does a spirited discussion in which there is a sharp difference of opinion turn into destructive quarreling? What fuels a quarrel more than anything else?

4. What sin do you think is at the root of suspicion? How do you think you can prevent suspicion from damaging the marital relationship?

5. What do you think is the best way to avoid physical and emotional exhaustion in your marriage?

Project

It's list time again. Over a quiet dinner, when both of you are unhurried, make a list of all the "debris" that has accumulated in your marriage. Discuss with your spouse how you can begin together to dispose of that debris. Be specific.

REWIRING THE COMMUNICATION

It was an innocent Tuesday evening call. As I entered the living room, I saw what appeared to be ten thousand wires lying in the middle of the floor going in hundreds of directions. That may be an exaggeration, but believe me when I tell you there were many wires. Most of them seemed to come from a common source which was the receiver of a two-way radio from a ship. I arrived at testing time, and the man whose family I had come to see was in another room testing the "rewired" project. When they turned the equipment on, we all heard at least ten messages going on at the same time and with the same volume. Whatever repair he had done to the equipment wasn't working. In the words of his wife, the radio was sending mixed messages. That was a mild way to put it. It was bedlam, to say the least. While all the messages from differing radio signals were loud and clear, they were competing with one another; and no one could decipher what was being said by anyone.

As I stood there and witnessed the confusion, I was suddenly reminded that this is a picture of what has happened to communication in well over fifty percent of marriages that are still intact.

No marriage repair kit would be complete without the intricate tools with which to do fine tuning in the communications department.

Carol and Stan were in need of those tools. The names are fictitious, but the couple isn't. I knew this couple only by sight at church, but had never really gotten to know them well. Stan invited me to lunch and before our salads came, he got right to the point. "I wanted to talk with you before I talk with the attorney. I can't take it any longer. Carol and I have decided to get a divorce. I know it's wrong, and that you won't agree . . . but when communication is over, the marriage is over."

Somehow when the salads came, I wasn't very hungry. I listened intently for another 35 minutes as he tried to explain the last three years of his fourteen-year marriage. In his words, they were like ships passing in the night. It was more than obvious that their marriage needed a total rewiring job in the area of communications. When the three-hour lunch "hour" was over, we had made an appointment for the three of us to get together. The rest is history, good history. After only a month, the lawyer's name was forgotten, the "rewiring" job was well underway, and this couple learned how to talk with one another again. No, it wasn't just that quick and simple, but some basic principles had to be set in place.

Lack of good communication can and does do a number on otherwise sound marriages. Somehow couples come to believe that because they live under the same roof, sleep in the same bed, eat at the same table, and have the same kids, communication will take care of itself. But good communication in marriage is like a garden. It isn't enough to plant it. It must be cultivated, weeded, fertilized, and pruned if it's going to survive and grow.

I'm sure we've all read this.

You didn't understand what I said, you only understood what you thought I said . . . in reality, you only thought you understood what you thought I said. The confusion came when what I thought you thought you understood, you really didn't understand at all, because what I thought you thought I thought I said was not really what I thought you thought about what I really said.

You can read that one hundred times and be more confused about the ninety-seventh time than you were the first. Yes, that is often the confusion that prevails in marital communication.

First of all we need to see the "communication robbers" that lurk in every marriage. As you read these, I'm sure you will spot some that have come to hinder your communication with your spouse.

False Assumption

"I just assumed you knew that we had no more money in our bank account when I didn't answer at all, and you went ahead and wrote a check anyway! How stupid can you get?"

Sound familiar? Sure does! That fiasco results from assuming too much. A good rule in the school of communications in marriage is this: DON'T ASSUME ANYTHING, ANYTIME.

Busy Schedule

Planning too many activities for a twenty-four hour day leaves no time to talk and communicate. We just assume that because we're busy, the spouse will automatically know what we want or mean. If you're too busy to sit down and talk with your spouse about family matters, schedules, work, school, friends, or whatever—you're too busy. Most couples fail to communicate because of this culprit.

Television and Newspapers

We've already spoken about the television problem. Suffice it to say at this point that before the tube is ever turned on in the evening, couples need to take a minimum of fifteen minutes to talk—even if it's nothing more than recalling how the day went. Also, you can't communicate when both of you are lost in a newspaper or magazine. We can have control over both, and we need to exercise that control.

Well-Meaning Friends

There is such a thing as having so many friends (albeit well-meaning friends), that they are consuming all of your waking hours. They're either over at your place, or they expect you to be over at their place. When the evening is done, there is little time left except to undress and collapse in a state of sleep so you can work the next day. Once again, communication has gone out the window.

Beware, because this is a subtle and quite "innocent" communication robber, but robber it is.

Exhaustion and Weariness

It happens when both partners work outside the home; it happens when only the man works outside the home and the wife works all day in the home. It's called, "Too tired to talk." The one thing you don't feel like doing when you're extremely tired is carrying on a meaningful conversation.

We can't avoid getting worn out at times. We can't always escape the "tired" syndrome because of work and pressure. But we need to make sure time is scheduled in when weariness and tiredness aren't part of our experience, when we're fresh and at our best. If you're exhausted every night of the week to the point that little or no communication is taking place, beware! You're in the danger zone!

Exhaustion doesn't just happen. There are some "energy robbers" with which we need to be familiar. One of the most common, especially among young marrieds, is excessive overtime at work by one or both partners. Young couples are particularly susceptible to this because their income is very limited this early in their life, and they really need all the overtime they can get. Be moderate in how much overtime you take on. Working ten or eleven hours per day for several days in a row can devastate your energy level, closing down communication.

Too much recreation and play can steal your energy. Every couple needs to crank into their schedule enough playtime, entertainment time, along with good physical exercise. But caution! Don't go overboard. Of course, hobbies can be good, but many couples find themselves in a frenzy of play activities until they have no time left to get to know and communicate with each other.

Hobbies can subtly consume time and energy so that you're exhausted making up lost time with other things that are essential. Hobbies are great and can even be stress reducers if you don't spend an inordinate amount of time on them. One woman recently told me her husband set up a workshop in the garage for a hobby, and she practically never saw him again. Every waking hour at home for months was spent carrying on a love affair with his drill press, bench saw, joiner, and sander! If a hobby is stealing your energy, cut back, or get rid of it altogether.

Another energy robber is imbalanced involvement in positions of responsibility at clubs, church, or neighborhood groups. Everyone should shoulder their share of the load, but some people have never learned to say "no." Because they are the willing ones, they soon become the burdened ones. One couple, living this kind of life with such involvement, found themselves home only one night out of the week. Reprehensible! That quickly brings on exhaustion, thus diminishing communication.

Beware, husbands, if your job causes you to travel: "Jet lag" causes you to lag, and a consistent diet of traveling on a regular basis can quickly strip you of energy.

Questions for Discussion

1. Be honest and objective even if it hurts. What do you feel is the biggest communication robber in you marriage?

2. Do you think there is any place for secrets in marriage, for example, withholding certain pieces of information from your spouse in order to avoid conflict?

3. Is it ever good to withhold angry feelings, or should they be expressed in a context of nonthreatening love and understanding? How can this be done? Think of how you would want to be treated.

4. Who generally has the greatest reluctance to communicate in a marriage, the wife or the husband? Why? What about in your marriage?

5. Is there such a thing as "overkill" in communication? Is it possible to talk too much? Why or why not?

Project

Husband: Make a date, set a time next week for you and your wife to be alone. Discussion topic: "What can I do to communicate better in the future?"

EIGHT

REWRITING THE BUDGET

In the state of Washington where I counsel there were over 11,000 divorces last year. Well over half of those divorces were directly or indirectly caused by major disagreements over money. It's almost like the wedding vows have been rewritten to read "until DEBT do us part."

The marriage machine will never hum with any kind of precision as long as conflicts exist over money. Long before couples "tie the knot," they need to understand the Biblical perspective of money. In some marriages, husbands don't trust their wives with money. In others, wives don't trust their husbands with money. The common complaint of men is that their wives don't understand how to live on their incomes. Wives are accused often of "living on the outskirts of their husband's income." And, of course, some do. On the other hand, many husbands provide their wives with only enough money to pay the basic bills of the household such as groceries, utilities, paper boy, and the like. Only that much and no more for her personal needs. Many wives are made to feel badly if they dare ask for a little extra money for a dress, shoes, or something for their personal needs.

There are some basic principles or rules every couple needs to know when it comes to money. Adherence to these principles may not guarantee financial prosperity, but it will keep conflict from occurring due to friction over money.

Jesus talked more about money and our relationship to it than he did Heaven, Hell, baptism, judgment, and the Second Coming—all put together. It's only when couples ignore the Biblical teaching that conflict enters the picture.

As Christians, We're Committed to Management Not Ownership.

Couples need to commit to this truth at the outset of marriage. We own nothing, we manage all. Jesus said,

> In the same way, any of you who does not give up everything he has cannot be my disciple (Luke 14:33).

Those are strong words. Some versions read "whoever does not renounce everything he has cannot be my disciple" (RSV). What does that mean? Does that mean when we accept Christ as our Savior, we must "turn over" all our possessions to Christ? No, it means we must ACKNOWLEDGE that we own nothing; that we hereby file a disclaimer to any personal property, and that we openly confess we don't own anything. In an age of great emphasis being placed on "things" and material prosperity, it's very difficult to disengage ourselves from material things. Virtually all Americans are afflicted with the disease known as "adoring the unpossessible." Jesus told a parable in Matthew 25 about a man who went on a journey and called his servants together to ENTRUST his property to them. Note, it didn't say he "gave" his property to them, but entrusted it to them. He gave differing amounts to different servants, each according to his ability. After he went away, he came back to "settle the accounts." The point of the parable is that God expects us to manage well what He has entrusted to us. There will be a day of accounting for us all.

The acknowledgement of God's ownership is not easy for us, yet the Scripture is clear at this point.

For every animal of the forest is mine, and the cattle on a thousand hills. I know every bird in the mountains, and the creatures of the field are mine. If I were hungry I would not tell you, for the world is mine and all that is in it (Psalm 50:10-12).

It changes our whole attitude toward money and material things when we realize we don't own them, but only manage them. It keeps us from becoming possessive and selfish. It also means that when God calls for those things, we don't have any problems releasing them.

When a couple marries, "mine" becomes "ours." We may have "his" and "hers" written on our towels in the bathroom, but it can't be written on our hearts in the marriage relationship. Everything is "God's," and we mutually become co-managers of what is His. This practically eliminates the need for the current trend toward prenuptial agreements. No matter what reason is given for these, the real issue is that each spouse is afraid the other will cheat him out of what is rightfully his in case of divorce.

No Secrets!

There is no place for secrets in marriage, especially when it comes to finances. If there is any place where openness and transparency need to prevail, it's in the financial department. Some husbands feel the need to conceal from their wives their salaries or how much they have in the bank. Some wives like to establish little "stash" accounts about which their husbands know nothing. Remember in marriage that the two have become one flesh. No secrets anymore, especially in the area of money. In cases where both spouses are working, it needs to be mutually agreed upon ahead of time how the wife's paycheck will be spent. Any over-time checks or special bonuses need to be divulged to one another.

Ban Separate Bank Accounts!

In counseling with a couple that was to be married, I discovered they planned to own property in their own names—separate cars, separate checking and savings accounts, and separate IRA accounts. They wanted the benefit of marriage, but desired to maintain separate identities in the name of having "space" even though married to each other. My suggestion was that they remain single! Separate bank accounts promote an independence and a nondependence on each other that is extremely dangerous in any marriage. It may presuppose a lack of trust in each other and tend to create reasons for arguments. As always, considered judgment needs to be used. Joint checking accounts, where both husband and wife can write checks, is the safest and most honest way to go.

Mandatory Budget—and Put God First!

If you aim at nothing you will surely hit it every time. If you try to live financially flying by the seat of your pants, you'll end up bankrupt. Every couple, regardless of the size of their income, probably could benefit from a budget. It doesn't have to be a budget down to the penny, but even a general budget will keep you out of financial "hot water." The items that are MUSTS in your budget include,

- Tithe
- Rent
- Auto
- Insurance
- Utilities
- Gifts
- Food

- Entertainment

- Clothes

- Miscellaneous (careful here)

Don't cheat on your budget. Don't rob Peter to pay Paul. Be careful about eating out often! It is extremely expensive, especially when you're on a very tight budget.

Avoid Shopping as a Hobby!

"Where are you going?" "Shopping." "For what?" "Nothing in particular, just shopping."

Sound familiar? That's a dangerous habit to acquire. Window shopping is fun and good for couples to do together. It's when they get inside the window that the danger begins. Here are some simple rules about shopping that can keep you within your budget at all times.

1. Determine exactly what you need before you head for the shopping mall. (Make sure it's a need, not just a want.)

2. Make phone calls to compare prices. This avoids wasting time and gas.

3. Ask yourself if a second-hand one rather than a new one will do as well and last as long.

4. Decide ahead of time the price limits and stick with them.

5. Make sure its purchase isn't going to overwork your budget for that week or month. If you don't have to have it NOW, wait a little longer.

6. Buy quality on most items, even if it costs a little more.

7. Never go grocery shopping without a list or on an empty stomach. Be sure to use coupons liberally.

8. AVOID KEEPING UP WITH THE JONESES!

Young couples can fall into this trap so easily. Another couple buys a piece of furniture, a car, a VCR, a camera, or whatever; and immediately they feel they need to go out and get one, too. Maybe even one that is a little better. Because we live in an affluent society where everything is geared to money, it's hard to extricate ourselves from the fiendish desire to acquire more and more.

God says we are to be content with what we have:

> But godliness with contentment is great gain. For we brought nothing into the world, and we can take nothing out of it. But if we have food and clothing, we will be content with that (1 Timothy 6:6-8).

Couples need to learn to live at the standard that is right for them—not falling prey to constant comparisons.

Have a Debt-Free Goal!

Debt has been a subtle wedge that splits many marriages apart. It is like a pall of gloom that settles over a marriage, literally crippling and paralyzing its health. Unmanageable debt creates resentment and bitterness that is hard to undo. Romans 13:8 says, "Let no debt remain outstanding, except the continuing debt to love one another." The Bible also teaches that "the borrower is servant to the lender" (Proverb 22:7). Many think if they can just "charge" it, somehow it will be easier to pay for later than now. This myth has ended many good marriages. My suggestion for all couples is to acquire a bank card of some kind to establish a good credit rating. But the rule is to never charge on that card what cannot be paid for in full when the statement comes in the mail. Stringing out the payments means paying interest rates, sometimes as high as 24 percent so that some items cost three or four times what they would have if they had been bought with cash. Of course, an item like a house that appreciates in value must be paid off on time, but items that depreciate should be paid for in cash if at all possible.

If you are in debt, don't incur any more debts until you've paid off what you owe. God doesn't want this strain on your marriage with all the other pressures you have.

Appoint a Head Bookkeeper!

Money decisions should be mutually decided upon, and a joint checking account needs to be in place. But the husband, as the head of the family, needs to either be the family bookkeeper or appoint his wife, if it isn't too great a burden to her and she is adept at figures. One person in the marriage needs to assume the responsibility of seeing that bills are paid on time and to supervise the budget so you know where the finances stand at all times.

Mutually Agree on Giving to God His Due!

Every couple needs to agree early in their marriage where God would have them give, then make sure that the first check written after payday is that check. The Bible suggests a starting figure of ten percent. The Bible gives a command and a promise that is hard to misunderstand.

> "Bring the whole tithe into the storehouse, that there may be food in my house. Test me in this," says the Lord Almighty, "and see if I will not throw open the floodgates of heaven and pour out so much blessing that you will not have room enough for it" (Malachi 3:10).

Ten percent of your gross salary is a good place to begin. Then as the Lord leads, you can raise it a percentage as God prospers. It is good to make sure that check is written first, before you begin to try to pay all the other bills.

Vote "No" for Working Wives!

This is a very sensitive subject, and I'm aware that some of you reading this book are single parents and have been forced into the work market to provide for yourselves and your children. This is indeed unfortunate, yet it is a reality with which we must live. We live in an economy that has forced some wives into the work place; but those cases, in reality, are rarer than many of us are willing to admit. Wives work outside the home for a number of reasons. Some work because their husbands have forced them to do so. How unfortunate! Men don't understand that they are merely "using" their wives in cases like this. Other women work so their families can enjoy a higher standard of living. This can be interpreted as a violation of Scripture that tells us to be content with what we have. Still other wives work because they are bored with being a mother and wife at home. Again, individual situations are complex, but many abrogate a God-given privilege. Other wives work with the design in view of pursuing a career.

If there are no children and the needs of the husband aren't being ignored, there is certainly nothing wrong with a woman working outside the home. But a mother with small children is desperately needed in the home. To delegate the raising of her God-given children to someone else nine hours per day can be a travesty, indeed, unless it is a complete necessity. Also, a spirit of independence develops that can be extremely detrimental. The wife is outside the covering of her husband's authority and protection, and thus becomes a candidate for temptations she otherwise wouldn't have. Of course, in cases of a husband's illness, or when he falls prey to extended layoffs, it may become necessary for a wife/mother to work. Even then, care should be taken for her to be home when her children come home from school or as much as possible.

Questions for Discussion

1. How much of a role does selfishness play in disagreements over money in marriage?

2. Should both partners always be in agreement before major purchases are made? Why or why not?

3. After the tithe is deducted, what takes priority in spending?

4. How can couples avoid the temptation to set their living standard higher than their income? What is the difference in wanting to better yourself—your house, your auto, your wardrobe—and covetousness?

5. Why do most couples fail to tithe from their income? What do you think are the Biblical instructions about giving?

Project

For spouses to do: If the wife is working fulltime, enumerate *all* the expenses required for her to work monthly. Include the following:

Extra clothes	$_____
Additional taxes	$_____
Increased auto expense	$_____
Meals out at work	$_____
Child care (if any)	$_____

Subtract these expenses from your monthly income, then ask, "Is it worth it?"

RELEASING THE PRESSURE

I wasn't prepared for the hot spray. My radiator had over-heated. I didn't know how much until I lifted the hood with handkerchief in hand and loosened the radiator cap. SWOOOOOSH! Out it came—fortunately for me I ducked, but hot boiling water mixed with anti-freeze went every-where. When the excitement settled, I read on the radiator cap in bold red letters, DO NOT OPEN WHEN PRESSURE HAS BUILT.

Good advice! It's excellent advice also for marriage. It is a given fact that pressure builds in marriage. While pressures change through the years and their causes vary, they have a way of building to the exploding point.

Causes of Pressure in Marriage

What are "pressure causes" in marriage? They are many and diverse. For newlyweds, there is just the pressure of the newness of it all—getting acquainted, learning how to live with a new "roommate," worrying about pleasing your new spouse, and the general pressure of being married rather than single. Add to that later the pressures of working, of deciding to have children, (then the pressure that comes when you do have them), of making enough money, of climbing the cor-porate ladder, of keeping a home, running a bank account, pleasing relatives, adjusting sexually . . . Where does the list end?

Of course, some pressures can be avoided. Some can't. The real question is how do we relieve the pressure which, if not relieved, can play havoc with the marriage?

Twelve Rules for a Happy Marriage

The following list has run the gamut of newspaper columns, church papers, and magazines; but no one seems to know who wrote it or has come up with a better set of guidelines. It's called the "TWELVE RULES FOR A HAPPY MARRIAGE."

1. Never both be angry at once.

2. Never yell at each other unless the house is on fire.

3. Yield to the wishes of the other as an exercise in self-discipline, if you can't think of a better one.

4. If you have a choice between making yourself or your mate look good, choose to make your mate look good.

5. If you feel you must criticize, do so lovingly.

6. Never bring up a mistake of the past.

7. Neglect the whole world rather than each other.

8. Never let the day end without saying at least one complimentary thing to your life's partner.

9. Never allow your life's partner to come home without an affectionate welcome.

10. Never go to bed mad.

11. As soon as you realize you've made a mistake, talk it out and ask sincerely for forgiveness.

12. Remember, it takes two to make an argument. The one who is wrong is the one who will be doing most of the talking.

Whoever wrote that, whether they know it or not, wrote helpful principles to prevent pressure from building in a marriage.

Love Releases the Pressure

Put in a Biblical perspective, the release of pressure only comes when a couple understands and puts into practice agape love as it is defined in 1 Corinthians 13. There, Paul, under the guidance of the Holy Spirit, defines what marital love is all about. Let's take a close look at it.

"Love is patient" (vs. 4). That means spouses aren't to tap their finger as they wait for a response. It knows how to wait, and wait some more, even for some much-needed changes.

"Love is kind" (vs. 4). Kindness is listed as one of the kinds of fruit of the Spirit (see Galatians 5:22-23). It means displaying or having a gentle spirit that treats the other person the way you would like to be treated.

"It does not envy" (vs. 4). We could almost say that the absence of envy in a marriage is the presence of love. Agape love is not interested in selfish envy of what the other has or is.

"It does not boast" (vs. 4). There is no place in a marital relationship for a boaster. Agape love doesn't "strut" and parade. It doesn't do self-stroking. It isn't a braggart. Boasting only drives a wedge between two people. We need to be like Paul who said, "May I never boast except in the cross of our Lord Jesus Christ" (Galatians 6:14). And John gave careful guidance when he said, "He [Jesus] must become greater; but I must become less" (John 3:30).

"It is not proud" (vs. 4). It is true that pride goes before destruction. Pride has destroyed more marriages than we can imagine, and usually it rears its ugly head in the male. Men somehow feel they have a "macho" image to maintain, and ego becomes everything. Pull the plug on pride or your matrimonial radiator will boil over!

"It is not rude" (vs. 5). Isn't it amazing that often married couples will be more polite to their boss, their neighbor, or a good friend than they will be to their mate? Rudeness takes on many forms—all the way from being curt over the phone, to terse and short answers when you are asked a question, to embarrassing your mate in front of others with harsh or critical words. Real agape love looks for ways to avoid rudeness and finds ways to treat others with great respect.

"It is not self-seeking" (vs. 5). Phillips' translation says, "It does not pursue selfish advantage." This is key in any marriage. If you're married for what you can get out of it, your radiator will constantly boil over. Narcissism (self-love) is the worst when expressed in a marital relationship. There is no room for contrivance in marriage, where one partner is constantly attempting to "stack the deck" to make the outcome beneficial for himself.

"It is not easily angered" (vs. 5). Again, J. B. Phillips has caught the real meaning of this little phrase when he translates, "It is not touchy." Agape love in marriage doesn't walk around "defensively." It's not wearing a chip on your shoulder and constantly daring the other to knock it off. There is a supersensitivity, better phrased as a "hypersensitivity," that has no place in a marriage. When no matter what your partner says to you, it sets you off in anger, you are hypersensitive and need to confess that to God and repent of it to Him and your partner.

"It keeps no record of wrongs" (vs. 5). When a hypercritical attitude prevails in either partner, pressure will build to more than just a boiling point. Agape love is not only forgiving, but it is forgetting. Bringing up past mistakes and offenses is like opening an old scar. Everytime it's opened, it takes longer to heal. Opened enough times, it won't heal. If you're going back weeks, months, or years and dredging up mistakes of the past, you are guaranteeing the demise of your marriage. Whether your notebook for recording the mistakes of your spouse is a little red one or a mental one, get rid of it!

The story goes that a troubled couple visited a marriage counselor. His advice to them was that every time one did something wrong, the other write it down and put it in a box. At the end of the month, they were to open the boxes to see who had the most wrongs. The time came. He opened his box to reveal all her mistakes. There were dozens recorded. She opened her box, and to his amazement some forty pieces of paper were there. On each was written, "I love you." It melted him and reconciliation came. He learned to stop criticizing her actions, and he learned to stop keeping a list of them.

"Love does not delight in evil" (vs. 6). That means true agape love doesn't cheer, whistle, and clap when the other partner makes a mistake or has a failure. Some married people love it when their partner slips up, bombs out, or caves in, because by contrast it makes them look good. One of your chief responsibilities in marriage is to constantly make your partner look good. Remember, love COVERS a multitude of sins. It doesn't expose them! Love, on the other hand, rejoices with the truth.

"It always Protects" (vs. 7). Love seeks to "cushion" your marriage partner from the bumps, abrasions, knocks, jars, and frictions that life brings. That doesn't mean that love tries to cover up truth or justify your spouse's mistakes to others. But it does imply that we're to develop a mutual "immune" system that looks out for the other person.

"Always trusts" (vs. 7). Trust isn't something we "have" in a marriage, it is something we show. Agape love doesn't have to go around like a detective with a magnifying glass "checking up" on the one we've married. It trusts (has full confidence in), always giving the other the benefit of the doubt. Suspicion in marriage is like a malignant tumor that goes untreated. It grows and grows, creating a pressure neither partner is equipped nor prepared to bear.

"Always hopes" (vs. 7). To hope is more than just to trust. It is to be optimistic about the other person. For many, optimism is missing in marriage. The light at the end of the tunnel for some is a locomotive coming full bore!

I heard recently a good definition of a pessimist. He is "one who feels bad when he feels good for fear he'll feel worse when he feels better!" Pessimism is more contagious than the latest "flu bug." It has a way of "rubbing off" on our marriage partner. So, to keep pressure from exploding in your face, practice hope. The Bible says, "And hope does not disappoint us" (Romans 5:5).

"Always perseveres" (vs. 7). Real agape love never "throws in the towel." Every divorce that occurs today is the result of someone throwing in the towel prematurely. We live in a society that quits everything too soon, marriage included. Because God doesn't give up on us, neither should we give up on our spouses, especially since we've married them for better and for worse.

"Love never fails" (vs. 8). What does this really mean? It means love is foolproof. So much that I own fails. My car may fail to start; my refrigerator may fail to get cool; my dishwasher may fail to get the dishes clean; my thermostat may fail my furnace; my mailman may fail to deliver mail; but love is "fail-proof." It always comes through and always works. When implemented, it has never recorded a failure. Agape love in a marriage is a most powerful force to be reckoned with. It's not that it has been tried and found wanting, but it has been tried and found difficult, then abandoned. Love never fails! Believe the Scriptures.

The Greatest of All

Faith is a wonderful thing. Hope is even more wonderful. But Paul said love is the greatest thing of all.

I learned a little verse in my early years of preparation for counseling. Its truth has proven true hundreds of times and every time.

He drew a circle that shut me out;
Heretic, rebel, a thing to flout,
But love and I had the wit to win.
We drew a circle that took him in.

That's powerful, and believe me, it works every time.

Are pressures building in your marriage? Release them by yielding to 1 Corinthians 13. It works every time. It matters not what's causing your pressure, whether it's financial, sexual, in-laws, whatever. Try administering love in large doses as defined on these pages. It works when nothing else will and guess what, NOTHING ELSE WILL!

Questions for Discussion

1. What do you feel is the greatest pressure for a married couple these days?

2. Who tends to get the blame in your marriage when you're under pressure?

3. In understanding agape love (unconditional commitment), why is it so difficult to manifest that commitment when the "feeling" of love is absent? How important is it to base our love on commitment rather than just on feelings for one another?

4. What are some practical ways you can discover your spouse's needs, then fulfill those needs to the best of your ability?

Project

For the couple: Read 1 Corinthians 13 together before retiring for bed every evening for seven straight days, BEGINNING TONIGHT. Make sure you read it from J. B. Phillips's translation if you have one. Pray together briefly before retiring, thanking God for one another.

REMODELING THE BEDROOM

In a watchmaker's window I saw the sign that read: ONLY TWO PEOPLE TAKE A WATCH APART. A FOOL AND A WATCHMAKER! That kind of statement may be said by someone about anyone who would dare to talk about sex in marriage; he's either a fool or an expert. I'm not really either.

Marital sex is a private thing between two people, and isn't to be "paraded" before the public nor made to be public conversation. Yet because so many marriages suffer in silence over this issue and because sex is a Biblical function, we can't leave it out.

The instructions that came in the plastic bag with my new power mower listed all the moving parts of the mower. When it came to the carburetor, it said in bold red letters: "WARN-ING: DELICATE ADJUSTMENTS WILL NEED TO BE MADE FOR SMOOTHER RUNNING." Not bad advice about sex in marriage.

Most couples communicate little about sex in marriage. Some are embarrassed, others are afraid they will offend their spouse if they make their needs known.

This chapter will not deal with techniques or biology. Rather, we will focus on the need to understand not only the purpose of sex from God's perspective, but to also under-stand that sex in marriage has been both minimized and over-emphasized by couples and by society. Though this is a book on repair, it must be said at this point that much of the repair in this department can be avoided if proper precaution is taken prior to marriage when it comes to sex.

Basically, God created sex, blessed it, ordained it, and said it was good — but ONLY within the confines of marriage. Thus, premarital sex is not only Biblically forbidden, it is emotionally devastating with destructive results often showing up much later.

If you're still single and reading this, please understand that to become involved sexually prior to marriage is to violate God's principle of purity. Plus it puts your life up for grabs by the spirit of lust. The Bible is clear:

> But among you there must not be even a hint of sexual immorality, or of any kind of impurity (Ephesians 5:3).

The word for immorality here is *porneia* in the Greek, which means adultery, fornication, homosexuality, bestiality, or any sex act committed outside the commitment of the marriage bond. Again,

> It is God's will that you should be holy; that you should avoid sexual immorality; that each of you should learn to control his own body in a way that is holy and honorable, not in passionate lust like the heathen, who do not know God (1 Thessalonians 4:3-5).

God wants you to come to the marriage bed clean and holy. If you have already made a mistake, confess it before God, turn away from immorality, and live a holy life. God will forgive your sexual sins of the past, but don't continue in those sins.

Couples who engage in premarital sex are far more likely to experience sexual dysfunction in marriage than couples who enter marriage as virgins.

What is the purpose of sex in marriage? Since God created it, sex is not only a physical function but a spiritual one. He confined its function to marriage; not because He wants to strip man of all his fun, but because He knows in His wisdom that its fulfillment can only come that way. Everything else is a cheap imitation of the real thing.

Sex Is for Intimacy in Marriage.

Genesis 2:18 says, "It is not good for the man to be alone. I will make a helper suitable for him." God had already allowed Adam to name all the animals He created but realized that he was lonely, incomplete, and, in a real sense, unfinished. "Suitable for him" in the Hebrew literally means "someone who fits perfectly." God's plan in bringing a woman into the picture for man was to bring him someone who would "fit" physically (hence, sex), emotionally, socially, mentally, and every other way. This tells me that woman was a "natural" for man. Sex without the commitment of intimacy is a cheap counterfeit—nothing more than the gratification of a physical drive.

Sex Is for Enjoyment and Mutual Pleasure.

No, it isn't wrong to say that. It was designed to be a fulfilling act, emotionally and physically for both the husband and the wife. While many marriages merely exist on the basis of the wife "enduring" the sex act so her husband can be satisfied physically, that is a poor substitute for what God originally designed.

When God caused a deep sleep to come upon Adam, took a rib, and from it formed a woman, He brought her to him. Adam's response when he saw his helpmate for the first time was: "WOW! THIS IS WHAT I'VE BEEN WAITING FOR!!" Well, that's not an exact translation, but he did say, "This is now bone of my bones and flesh of my flesh" (Genesis 2:23). What does that mean? It means Eve was made of the same "stuff," the same "components," that Adam was with one unique difference. She was a woman while he was a man. Not only were they physically created different, their whole psyche was different, yet complementary. Then comes the pleasure part of sex.

> For this reason a man will leave his father and mother and be united to his wife, and they will become one flesh (Genesis 2:24).

This "one flesh" is, I concede, a spiritual union between two people; but it is symbolically guaranteed by the intimacy of the sex act, coitus or intercourse. First Corinthians 6:16 tells us that intercourse is becoming one flesh with the one with whom that takes place.

While sex is for personal pleasure, you need to be warned that not every sexual encounter is a super experience. Every couple goes through the "humdrums" of sex, and like anything, it can become quite ordinary and even dull at times. Sex in the bedroom doesn't begin there, but may start in the kitchen with a hug and kiss, along with tender words.

Sex Is for Having Children.

It is, in fact, commanded, "Be fruitful and increase in number; fill the earth and subdue it" (Genesis 1:28). Human reproduction is a reason for sex. In our narcissistic age, when many couples are opting out of having children, we need to remember that one of the purposes of getting married is to have children. That is the godly thing to do.

Couples who are choosing not to have children today need to reread what God said about children:

Sons are a heritage from the Lord, children a reward from him. Like arrows in the hands of a warrior are sons born in one's youth. Blessed is the man whose quiver is full of them (Psalm 127:3-5).

God plans differing numbers of "arrows" for different couples, but to avoid having children altogether is disobedience to God.

One of the most important things I have told couples coming to get married is that once married, their bodies no longer belong to them. Of course they always belong to God; but marriage suggests that once the commitment is made in that relationship, their bodies belong to each other.

The Scriptures bear this out:

The husband should fulfill his marital duty to his wife, and likewise the wife to her husband. The wife's body does not belong to her alone but also to her husband. In the same way, the husband's body does not belong to him alone but also to his wife (1 Corinthians 7:3-4).

What this means is that there must be a mutual sharing and unselfishness when it comes to sex. Paul goes on to say in that same passage:

Do not deprive each other except by mutual consent and for a time, so that you may devote yourselves to prayer. Then come together again so that Satan will not tempt you because of your lack of self-control (1 Corinthians 7:5).

It is vital at this point to explain the difference between male and female. There is a difference! They not only look different, talk differently, act differently, plan differently, think differently—they feel differently.

While there are many similarities in a man's and a woman's being, we need to dwell here on the differences in their needs. A woman's needs are for emotional support and security. They are not necessarily "turned on" by a man's body, though they too are attracted somewhat by physical appearance. A kiss, a hug, and some words of understanding greatly satisfy a woman's needs much more than just the physical sex act. A man, on the other hand, is far more physical. For him there is great physical and emotional gratification in the sex act, and he is more stimulated by the physical sight of his wife's body than she is by his.

None of this is to suggest that women don't need physical satisfaction and orgasms in sex. It is only to suggest that physical satisfaction tends to be a specific need more so for the man than the woman. The woman's needs are just as great but satisfied differently.

Maybe the activity in your bedroom has gone sour. Delores was experiencing this. Into marriage only five months, she came to say that it wasn't what she expected. The sex was a great thing for her husband, but a "chore" for her. Of course, her low interest in it affected his fulfillment as well, and things weren't going smoothly at all! What she had expected and what she was experiencing turned out to be two different things. After talking with her, then the two together, I discovered they had both violated some important principles of sex in marriage. Their bedroom desperately needed a remodeling job.

If sex in your marriage has become bland—a chore, routine, mechanical, and perfunctory—apply these rules.

Recommit Yourself and Your Body Again to Jesus Christ.

"Do not offer the parts of your body to sin, as instruments of wickedness, but rather offer yourselves to God, as those who have been brought from death to life" (Romans 6:13).

Remember, you are not your own; you are bought with a price.

Remember that Your Body Belongs to Your Mate.

As we have already noticed in 1 Corinthians 7:3, once married, you turn your body over to your mate. It's not all yours anymore.

Talk Freely to Each Other about Your Sexual Frustrations.

Lack of communication at this level can bring about frustrations that can build and build until they become highly destructive to the marriage. Agree now with each other that there is nothing so intimate and private that you will not be willing to discuss with each other, even at the risk of offending the other. Though this may be difficult, talk about problems in love, not in threats.

Settle Conflicts in Other Areas Before Having Sex.

Some couples believe they can have an argument at the dinner table, continue to threaten and intimidate all evening, then jump into bed. Just because both are lying there, suddenly they expect a magical change in feeling so they can perform sexually. Wrong! That's perhaps a reason why the Bible tells us to not let the sun go down on our anger. Sex is not a magic formula that erases all your differences. If you disagree about the kids prior to sex, that same disagreement will be there after sex.

Don't Use Withholding Sex as a Club to Get Your Way.

Often either the husband or the wife will withhold sex until they get what they want in another area. Apart from being ungodly, this is damaging to your relationship as husband and wife and can be emotionally disturbing in your sex life. God never authorized sex as a "club" to be used by either spouse to manipulate their way. Actually, Scripture makes this abundantly clear as we have already seen.

> The husband should fulfill his marital duty to his wife, and likewise the wife to her husband. The wife's body does not belong to her alone but also to her husband. In the same way, the husband's body does not belong to him alone, but also to his wife. Do not deprive each other except by mutual consent and for a time, so that you may devote yourselves to prayer (1 Corinthians 7:3-5a).

Sex in marriage confirms an intimacy. It emotionally and physically carries out that intimacy. To withhold sex in order to get your way or to yield your body as bargaining collateral is to cheapen and prostitute it. The Bible makes it abundantly clear in more than one place that we are not to look to our own interests, but also to the interests of others.

See the Sex Act as an Act of Giving, not Receiving.

If narcissism is rampant anywhere, it's in marriage, especially the sex department! If you are approaching lovemaking wholly on the basis of the gratification of your glandular needs, it's doubtful whether your sexual relationship with your partner will ever be fulfilled. It's not, "What can I have, and how soon can I get it?" but "What can I give, and how can I meet (his/her) need?" This goes back to what we spoke about earlier. At no place in Scripture do we see a list of expectations we're told to look for, but rather a list of instructions we're told to do.

This is not to deny a God-given physical and emotional need both men and women have sexually. And yes, I'm very much aware that a physical and emotional climax for both husband and wife releases a pressure that has been building. Be all of that as it may, we still need to approach lovemaking as a giving act. Of course, a great benefit to that kind of approach is that we usually receive far more than we give. It's like the worship of God. Worship is always God-ward. We don't enter into worship for what we can get out of it, but for the glorification of God. Yet in the process of giving to Him our praise and adoration, we come away greatly enriched.

No marriage partner should ever be viewed as a "sex object" to be used, but rather as a love object to be loved. And ladies, though your husband is often considered to be the "initiator" in sex, there is a lot of giving you need to do before coitus actually begins. You're not simply to be there as an "object of his conquest" but as a willing, giving, loving partner who responds with warmth and acceptance. Of course, husbands are to be willing, giving, and loving too. Love always gives, lust always takes. This is why premarital sex is a perversion of the real thing God planned. When a man says to a woman, "If you really love me, you'll have sex with me," what he's really saying is, "I want to use you to satisfy and gratify my own needs here at the moment." This is the epitome of selfishness. But beware! Just because you're married doesn't exempt you from this selfish attitude. It may be old and seem trite, but it's so true—it's Jesus, others, and you. Nowhere does this apply more than in marriage, especially in the bedroom.

Keep the Intimacy of Your Marital Sex a Private Thing.

More damage has been done in this area than should ever be. Part of the special relationship between married partners is the privacy of their marriage. What is done and said in the bookkeeping room shouldn't be broadcast to others, even to the best of friends. By the same token, what is said and done in the bedroom shouldn't be discussed with others unless there is a particular need for counseling. It's between the two of you alone, and no one else. When this confidence and privacy is destroyed, a betrayal takes place that is difficult, some-

times almost impossible, to heal. Some think by discussing
with close friends such things as "methods," "techniques,"
"frequency," and the like they can get advice on how to im-
prove their sex life. Not so. In fact, in reality what it really
does is make something that God meant to be precious and
private, open and cheap. Confine your discussions about
your bedroom activity to each other.

Do Nothing Sexually that Is Against Your Spouse's Scruples.

There is much discussion in this day of "open sex" concerning what is admissible and nonadmissible for married
partners. This basically revolves around the rightness or
wrongness of oral sex. Biblically, there is no precedent for or
against it. This rule of thumb may be helpful: *Anything* is
permissible in a marital physical relationship that doesn't violate either spouse's conscience.

In other words, both partners must be completely comfortable with and approving of an act in order for it to be "all
right." Suppose a husband is perfectly comfortable with oral
sex, but the wife is far from at peace with it. Then it shouldn't
be done. No technique or act should ever be forced upon the
other. To do so violates the Scriptural injunction to walk in
love. This is why communication is so important in marriage,
especially in the sexual department. Many husbands brow-
beat their wives at this point in their relationship. They feel
that because they are the "head" (they think of being "boss"
rather than being servant) of the marriage and that because
the wife is to be in submission to them, they have a "right" to
be gratified any way they want sexually. Sorry men, but the
minute you fall prey to that attitude, a selfishness has entered
into your marriage that will ultimately destroy, or at least
greatly damage your marriage.

Avoid All Artificial Eroticism to Stimulate Your Sex Life.

Translated into plain English, this means to avoid all forms of pornography. While ninety-five percent of this warning goes to men, wives need to heed this as well. Pornography is destroying many marriages in our nation today. It is a mental form of adultery that is so subtle. Even some Christians get involved.

Today, many secular sex therapists abound. Their advice to revive lagging sex in a marriage often is to use "visual stimulation." That is usually in the form of porno movies, objects, or magazines. I cannot remember how many women have told me their husbands are regular users of pornography; and when confronted, they piously justify their involvement by convincing their wives it's really for their benefit.

Pornography is diametrically opposed to God's plan for fulfillment sexually in marriage. It twists and perverts God's best into that which is not natural, and thus is used by Satan effectively to bring incompatibility in the sex department of marriage. This is one point where I believe there is no room for negotiation. Whichever partner is involved in pornography (and it is usually the husband) needs to be confronted and informed: This is not acceptable! Avoid it like the plague!

**Stay Sexually True to Your Partner
Both Mentally and Physically.**

You might think, "Does that really need to be said? Isn't it just assumed?" Yes, it needs to be said and repeated many times, even to those who profess a relationship with Christ.

We live in a day when the moral boundary lines are being moved all the time to accommodate lifestyles. The moral absolutes of thirty years ago are obsolete in most circles. The new morality and doctrine of open sex have as their motto: IF IT FEELS GOOD, DO IT. Oh, they will often attempt to "sanctify" their campaign by saying "If it's 'meaningful,' it's all right," even if the parties involved are not married. I never cease to be amazed at what lengths people go to justify immorality. Does the Bible really teach that adultery is wrong? Paul uses an interesting word in Ephesians 5.

> But among you there must not be even a hint of sexual immorality, or of any kind of impurity, or of greed, because these are improper for God's holy people (Ephesians 5:3).

The word he uses for immorality is the Greek word "porneia." It means any sex act that is not within the confines of marriage. It includes extramarital sex (adultery), premarital sex (fornication), homosexuality, bestiality, and the like. God forbids sexual relations outside of marriage.

Latest statistics reveal that over 40 percent of all married men have sex outside of marriage at least once. How tragic! Of that 40 percent, some 90 percent of their spouses don't know it. But know it or not, it shows up sooner or later, taking its toll on their marriage. True, a marriage ripped apart by adultery can be healed and repaired, but something is stolen that can never be replaced.

Mental adultery also occurs, causing just as much devastation as physical adultery. It's called "fantasizing." While both men and women are involved in this mental game, it occurs more among men than women. This erotic daydreaming (and some would include night dreaming) creates mental pictures of sexual encounters with other partners besides one's spouse. Since we become what we think, sexual fantasizing has made adulterers of many.

How can you avoid this mind game? I believe there's only one way that is effective. It's found in Colossians 3:1-2:

> Since, then, you have been raised with Christ, set your hearts [minds] on things above, where Christ is seated at the right hand of God. Set you minds on things above, not on earthly things (Colossians 3:1-2).

How do you do that? Since we're the ones who control our thoughts, we do it by a deliberate act of the will. This isn't to say there won't be times when those fantasies suddenly appear without warning. But we don't have to throw out the welcome mat for them. In fact, we need to let them know how unwelcome they really are. This comes only by a renewal of the mind, which the Scripture talks about so much.

How do you renew the mind? By having all your thoughts pass through the sieve of the Word of God. That's why it is so essential that wives and husbands get into God's Word on a daily basis, believing God for the purity of their marriages in thought and deed. It can be done, and many are doing it. What about you?

I don't know who first penned this, but it's true:

Sow a thought, and reap a deed;
Sow a deed, and reap a character;
Sow a character and reap a life;
Sow a life and reap a destiny.

Delores and her husband eventually found fulfillment as they both adopted and owned these basic principles. It can happen to you also if you're willing.

I used to wonder what the writer of Hebrews meant when he talked about "and the marriage bed kept pure" (Hebrews 13:4). Now I think I know. We need to follow God's guidelines; they work every time. Nowhere is this more true than in the bedroom. Go ahead, redecorate your bedroom. You'll be glad you did!

Questions for Discussion

1. Why do you think sexual hang-ups are on the increase in marriages of young couples today?

2. Do you think a husband has the right to "demand" sex whether the wife is agreeable or not? Why or why not?

3. Why do you think couples have more communication problems in the sexual area than any other area of marriage?

4. Why is sex prior to marriage with the one you are to
   marry a damaging thing? (Remember, if this occurred
   with you, it is forgivable by God. But it takes prayer and
   patience to work through the consequences.)

5. What is the basic difference between a man's sexual need
   and a woman's? Why is it that often neither one is satisfied?

Project

For the couple: Answer the following questions on paper,
then have a time to discuss privately with each other:

1. What is my biggest fear in sex?

2. What would you like me to do to make our sex life more
   meaningful and fulfilling?

3. What am I doing or not doing that is causing tension in
   this area?

4. What would you suggest for both of us to make our sexual encounters more meaningful?

RESUMING THE CHILDLESS YEARS

It's only appropriate to make the final chapter focus on the final years of a marriage. I believe that it is not over-simplifying the matter to say that the main three phases of any marriage are ALONE, INVADED, then ALONE AGAIN.

It's true. Couples marry and enjoy a year or two without children. Everything is planned around two—two places at the table, two towels in the bathroom, two cars in the garage, two toothbrushes in the rack, two closets in the bedroom. Life is relatively simple at this stage.

Then baby comes! Crash, bam, shazam! The calm tranquility is invaded with crescendo. It's more than "Just Molly and me, and baby makes three." An amazing thing happens when a baby comes. A great amount of affection, energy, enthusiasm, time, and money, all of a sudden, get redirected . . . from each other to the baby.

Then comes another baby. All of that time, energy, affection, and enthusiasm is filtered yet again. It isn't that the couple stops loving each other; it isn't that they have nothing left for each other. But to say it doesn't change is to have your head in the sand. It does, sometimes drastically, as you who have children can testify.

Soon, plans begin to revolve around the child or children. As they get older, this intensifies. Times alone with just each other as a married couple become rarer and rarer. In fact, to actually take the time and spend it alone often brings a twinge of guilt, especially to the mom. Before we know it, most of our attention is focused on the kids. During the adolescent years (and nowadays long before) the mom becomes a short-order cook, taxi driver, laundry lady, and the official keeper of schedules on the kitchen calendar. It's a full-time job, with much of it centered not on the spouse, but on the kids.

I'm not suggesting this is bad, or even unnatural. It comes with the "turf." But I've known few couples who prepare for the years when the last child is gone, and they return to the "alone years" again. Most don't even think about that, because they have neither the time nor energy!

Not much has been said or written about this crucial time, even though it is probably the most crucial time in any marriage.

The scenario usually looks like this. Here's a family with three children. After high school, they're in and out of college, in and out of the house. Even those who don't attend college might get their own place, then return home or send their laundry home. Most of the time the break from home doesn't come easily. Economics often see to that. But then comes that summer or fall when the last child makes the final move out—either because of marriage, or moving to another city, or both. We don't really prepare for it; it suddenly is upon us; and we're nowhere near ready.

One man told me that the first morning his last son was married and gone for good, he and his wife sat at the breakfast table alone for the first time in twenty-four years, and he said, "Have we met?" While they both laughed, they soon discovered in the days ahead it was good that they laughed. They really wanted to cry—not just over the fact that their kids were now raised and gone, but because they both knew that their number one priority was getting reacquainted with each other. Suddenly all that energy and affection that had been redirected twenty-four years earlier was now being rerouted again back to each other. "We weren't prepared for it in the least," he told me.

While this can't really qualify as something that needs repairing in marriage, it does need attention and lots of it.

The later empty-nest years can be both bane and blessing. It's really up to the couple. Their first step must be the admission that there will be an adjustment, no matter how much planning and preparation are made for that time. The romantic poetry of "come and grow old with me, the best is yet to be" is only true as we work at it and determine to make it work.

In order to resume those years with the least amount of pain and disruption, the following steps need to be observed with tenacity.

Talk About It Much Before It Ever Happens.

Many couples go through a form of denial during this time of their lives. They live and talk as though this time will never come. Denied or not, it comes! Many have found it helpful to talk openly about it while the last child is still at home and perhaps for as much as a whole year before they plan to leave.

Some subjects that should be covered are "What will we do? How will we use all the extra room? How will our lifestyle change? How will we handle it when they want to come home to live again?" (Most of them will at least once.) These are all questions which wise couples will openly discuss, even in the presence of their child or children. This greatly takes the edge off when it does occur. While firm plans don't need to be made early on, some options need to be considered.

Sit Down Together and Readjust Your Budget.

While you may not feel the difference immediately, there is usually an adjustment to the amount of money you'll have going out (after all the wedding bills are paid!). While it may not seem like having the last child move out would affect your budget, it does. And while most parents financially help their kids in those first months and years of separation, there is still a considerable difference in your budget from when they lived at home and when they moved away.

You no longer are buying their clothes. Utility bills should decrease some. They may go off your health and auto insurance; your food bill should decrease some; and perhaps college payments will decrease or stop. The average couple with their last child leaving home could realize anywhere from $50 to $150 per month they're no longer paying out. Something constructive which you mutually agree upon needs to be done with those funds. This demands taking the time to sit down and intelligently discuss it until some decisions can be reached.

You may opt to put it into an account for the grandkids; you may opt to give $75 a month to your child to help with expenses when he first moves away. Some stash this extra away for their 25th or 30th anniversary that occurs soon or shortly after this time. The worse thing to do is nothing, so that you end up carelessly blowing that money on this and that.

Don't Hinder the Separation Process.

Let your child go! Even if he is the last one, and especially because he is the last one. Some couples think they're doing their children a favor by encouraging them not to leave the household, even for two or three years after they have finished college. Don't stand in their way, neither give them the impression that you can't wait for them to leave. This is not an easy time for them either. Establishing their independence can be a very painful, slow process. This is no time for doting over your children, even if you do have feelings of panic or loneliness that they are leaving. They need to know it's all right with you if they leave and that it's all right with you if they stay.

It's natural for them to go, yet many young people feel a twinge of guilt about leaving, especially if they're needed for economic reasons. Assure them that it's the right thing to do, no matter how it may hurt to see them go. A farewell "cry" is always in order. Some couples don't cry until later—or not at all. We cried each time our three children left for good.

The key rule of thumb here is to let nature take its course. Never make your children feel bad nor lay on the guilt. They are doing a very natural thing by leaving.

Be Sensible About Confining Your Friendships with Your Grown Children.

Of course you want your kids to come home and visit, and you want to visit them. Be careful, however, that you don't wear out your welcome and don't allow them to do the same. So many spouses in the later childless years overdo at this point by spending all their evenings and week-ends with their grown children; or they insist that they spend all their social time with them. To be sure, it's vitally important to stay in touch and visit each other often. No family that has been close can avoid this, nor should any family.

But there is an inherent danger here for parents to restrict their friendships by confining their circle of friends only to their grown-up, moved-away children. If your children move away to another city, this problem is fairly well solved by distance. When they live in the same town, it's much easier to fall into this trap.

It's important for daughters to keep in touch daily with their moms for tips and helps in homemaking, mothering, and other domestic activities. But watch out parents! Don't overdo it. If your children do move away and you visit them, make your visits fairly brief, not for weeks at a time. It's better for you to leave when they're insisting that you stay longer than to stay longer while they're wishing you would "head home." Don't wear out your welcome.

Now is your chance to develop some friendships with other couples in the same boat. No need for baby-sitters anymore; no need of settling the car issue every evening. You're free to go and have a good time with people your own age and interest. Resuming the "childless" years opens up a whole new vista of friendship possibilities for you that were not there when the children were still at home.

Avoid Hobbies That Drive You Apart Instead of Bringing You Together.

Many couples fall into the subtle trap of taking up individual hobbies (which in themselves aren't bad) when their last child is gone, but individual hobbies can drive them away from each other instead of bringing them together. Without denying the need for individuality during these years, it is important that you try to do more things together than separately. Some take up square dancing, golfing, bicycling, jogging, fishing, swimming, or skydiving. The diversion you pick isn't nearly as important as it is to do it together. Some men start taking their wives with them on their business trips, just to be with them more than before. Some couples do a side business together, not so much for the money, but for the togetherness. What is important is that you're doing something together, regardless of how many things you do apart.

Commit Yourselves to a Mutual Ministry.

Now as never before, you have the opportunity to do a ministry together in your church. When the children were home, you usually had to do your ministry apart from each other. Now is your opportunity to find something the two of you can do, and like to do, together. It may be taking on a home fellowship, teaching a class, serving as greeters, singing in the choir, serving in the nursery or preschool. Whatever it is, make it a team effort. This has more "binding" power for one another than anything else.

It's much easier to do this now since you don't have to get home at a certain time. You can eat your evening meal when you desire; you don't have your children's schedule to meet anymore.

Because the average age of couples who resume their childless years has been about 42 to 50, some couples have found a real ministry in assisting young couples in their marriages — serving as lay-counselors and as an "ear" for those in their first few years of marriage. If there were more of this, we would certainly see many fewer divorces than we do.

So, find a ministry and get involved in it with each other.

Spend Time Firming Up Your Objectives and Goals for the Future.

This is a place where many couples miss it. Most couples are only ten to twenty years away from active retirement when the last child leaves home. With some retiring at 55 today, such people are closer than that. It's time to sit down and begin firming up plans for that time. Those plans don't have to be set in concrete, but some things ought to be settled. Where will you live in those years? How much (or little) will you be required to live on? What are some things you both want to do in those years before you grow too old to enjoy them. What steps need to be taken NOW to prepare more thoroughly for those years? It's easy to "fly by the seat of your pants" when it comes to facing retirement years; yet it's a proven fact, the couple who fails to plan at this point plans to fail.

One couple told me that the day their last child left home, they opened up a "dream and wish" file in their desk. As they thought about things they would like to do in the future, they dropped them in that file. Once a month they had a special dinner out and brought along those plans to discuss. Some they kept, some they tossed away; but at least they were talking, planning, dreaming, and anticipating.

Since half the fun of the trip is in going and not just getting there, so more than half the fun of retirement is in planning for it, saving for it, and anticipating the time. Now that so many time demands concerning the raising of the kids are off you, you have more time to sit and firm up those plans for tomorrow.

Pay Close Attention to Your Health.

The "childless" years happen to be that particular time of life when physical check-ups become more and more important. The years between forty and fifty are often years when ill-health is likely to occur. It is during this time that it becomes essential for the woman to be checked regularly for cancer of the cervix and breast, the two most common breeding grounds in women for the dread disease. This decade is crucial also for men to get frequent tread-mill tests for their hearts as well as consistent prostate check-ups.

Be careful here that you don't go to extremes and become overly concerned about your health. This is also the age when hypochondria occurs more than at any other age. God doesn't want us worried constantly about our health. It does, however, become extremely important that we watch our cholesterol intake and get the proper amount of physical exercise. It doesn't mean at 45 we're falling apart or getting old, especially in this culture where people are living much longer. What it does mean, though, is that we need to be wise enough to know that "an ounce of prevention is worth many pounds of cure." It's much easier to ward off a heart attack by diet and exercise than to recover from a massive heart attack or even by-pass surgery.

Our bodies are the temples of the Holy Spirit; and as they get older, they need more frequent inspections. God certainly doesn't want us "obsessed" with health, but He does want us concerned enough to place ourselves under the medical search-light for the revealing of problems, which multiply as we get older.

If your spouse hasn't become your best friend by the time your last child has left home . . . now is a good time for that to happen. Resuming the "childless" years can be either a night-mare, fraught with impossible adjustment barriers, or it can be a fun time when being partners takes on new dimensions.

Every man might want to pray this prayer after his last child is gone:

> Dear God, I'm alone again with my wife after 24 years. Help me to make these the very best years. Reorder my schedule to include her more and more. Redirect my think-ing to remember little things to do for her . . . help me not to get in the way, but also prompt me to be present more than I've been in the past. Lord, I know that she's not needed in exactly the same way she was, so help me to help her know she's needed in new ways . . . as never before. Lord, apart from you, make her the number one priority of my life, in my speech, my calendar, my checkbook, and my prayers. O Lord, draw us together as never before, and may the last quarter century of our life be even more precious than the first one. Amen.

Conclusion

I hope you have found the tools in this repair kit helpful for your own marriage. Though certainly not exhaustive, these tidbits were meant to help you *adjust* those areas of your marriage that need some adjustment. We're not talking about radical surgery, but a fine-tuning process to make the motor of your marriage run much more smoothly.

Keep the following Ten Commandments for marriage at hand. They may prove helpful and a blessing for your future years, that they may be even better than the past.

Ten Commandments for A Happy Marriage

1. Thou shalt have no other task before thee as important as honoring thy spouse.

2. Thou shalt love thy spouse with unconditional surrender till death do thee part.

3. Thou shalt never fail to communicate with thy spouse regardless of how difficult it may seem.

4. Thou shalt always remember thy spouse's birthday and wedding anniversary.

5. Thou shalt pray for thy spouse daily.

6. Thou shalt not allow the sun to go down while angry with thy spouse.

7. Thou shalt remember to speak at least one compliment per day to thy spouse as long as thou livest.

8. Thou shalt never allow thy spouse to guess where he/she stands in thy pecking order of priorities.

9. Thou shalt do all thou canst to protect thy spouse from the harsh things of this life.

10. Thou shalt spend all the quality time thou can with thy spouse.

Amen.

Questions for Discussion

1. What things can be done now to insure closeness when the empty-nest time comes?

2. Discuss what you think ought to be the proper attitude of parents toward children who are grown and out on their own?

3. What do you think is the difference between selfishness and a couple's desire to spend time alone without including their grown children? Explain.

Project

For couples and grown children: Hold an informal "congress" with your grown children, a frank discussion on how the relationships have changed, so together you can best express the new relationships. This needs to include policies on loans, frequency of visits, and the like. Get everyone to express their true feelings in a nonthreatening atmosphere.

COLOPHON

The typeface for the text of this book is *Sabon*, the one significant typeface created by the well-known typographer, Jan Tschichold. In the early 1960s a group of German printers decided they needed a type which could be set on Monotype or Linotype equipment, or in a foundry version by hand, with no perceptible difference on the page. This meant that all the drawbacks of both composing machines, the Monotype unit width grid and the Linotype's inability to kern, had to be resolved in a design which should look, the specification said, like a Garamond made a whisker narrower for economy's sake. Tschichold rose to the challenge with an astonishing professionalism for someone better known as a user rather than a creator of typefaces. Completed in 1966, his design is an admirable face, strong and yet restrained. Though it is a variation of Garamond, it has only a hint of Garamond about it. It is named after Jacob Sabon, a punchcutter from Lyon, who is thought to have brought some of Garamond's matrices to Frankfurt.

Substantive editing by Barbara Sorensen
Copy editing by Stephen Hines
Cover design by Kent Puckett Associates, Atlanta, Georgia
Typography by Thoburn Press, Tyler, Texas
Printed and bound by Maple-Vail Book Manufacturing Group
Manchester, Pennsylvania
Cover Printing by Weber Graphics, Chicago, Illinois